# What's the Evidence?

This book gives an account of a recent study into the nature of teacher quality that moves beyond typical discussions of teacher impact on student results and into what it means to be a teacher.

It describes how a range of different research methodologies were combined to design a process for research-informed examinations of teacher quality and the predictive validity of teaching performance assessments. The authors present qualitative and quantitative evidence that reveals how education stakeholders including teachers perceive what teacher quality is and what it might look like in the classroom. They aim to shift the discourse on this issue by changing the language we use to talk about teachers and what they do. In re-examining how we think about teachers, this work highlights the complex nature of defining teacher quality and what is required for successful engagement in the profession.

Putting forth a new understanding of teacher quality, this is an essential resource for education academics and students, as well as teaching professionals. Further information about the study discussed in this book is available at https://www.sydney.edu.au/arts/our-research/research-projects/teacher-quality/whats-the-evidence.html.

**Rachel White** is a senior lecturer at Western Sydney University, Australia. Her discipline is music education, with broader teaching and research interests in gifted education, educational psychology, and the creative arts.

**Alyson Simpson** is a Professor of Education at the University of Sydney, Australia. Specialising in English and Literacy Education, she works with pre-service teachers in Undergraduate and Graduate-entry programs. She is also an international expert in dialogic learning and lead investigator on the What's the Evidence? project funded by the NSW Department of Education.

# What's the Evidence?
## An Investigation into Teacher Quality

**Edited by Rachel White
and Alyson Simpson**

First published 2025
by Routledge
4 Park Square, Milton Park, Abingdon, Oxon OX14 4RN

and by Routledge
605 Third Avenue, New York, NY 10158

*Routledge is an imprint of the Taylor & Francis Group, an informa business*



*British Library Cataloguing-in-Publication Data*
A catalogue record for this book is available from the British Library

*Library of Congress Cataloging-in-Publication Data*
Names: White, Rachel (Writer on education), editor. | Simpson, Alyson, editor.
Title: What's the evidence? : An investigation into teacher quality / edited by Rachel White and Alyson Simpson.
Description: Abingdon, Oxon ; New York, NY : Routledge, 2025. | Includes bibliographical references and index.
Identifiers: LCCN 2024062036 (print) | LCCN 2024062037 (ebook) | ISBN 9781032893952 (hardback) | ISBN 9781032893969 (paperback) | ISBN 9781003542575 (ebook)
Subjects: LCSH: Teacher effectiveness. | Teachers--Rating of. | Teaching--Evaluation.
Classification: LCC LB2838 .W493 2025 (print) | LCC LB2838 (ebook) | DDC 371.102--dc23/eng/20250128
LC record available at https://lccn.loc.gov/2024062036
LC ebook record available at https://lccn.loc.gov/2024062037

ISBN: 978-1-032-89395-2 (hbk)
ISBN: 978-1-032-89396-9 (pbk)
ISBN: 978-1-003-54257-5 (ebk)

DOI: 10.4324/9781003542575

Typeset in Times New Roman
by SPi Technologies India Pvt Ltd (Straive)

# Contents

# Contributors

**Janet Clinton** is a Professor in Evaluation, Deputy Dean of the Melbourne Graduate School of Education, and the Director of the Teacher and Teaching Effectiveness Research Hub at the University of Melbourne, Australia.

**Wayne Cotton** is an Associate Professor in the Sydney School of Education and Social Work, The University of Sydney, Australia.

**Christopher Day** is a Professor of Education and member of the Centre for Research on Educational Leadership and Management at the University of Nottingham, United Kingdom.

**Chris Freeman** is an academic with the Centre for Educational Measurement and Assessment at the University of Sydney, Australia.

**George Harb** is a Lecturer in the Faculty of Arts and Social Sciences at the University of Technology Sydney, Australia.

**Nicole Hart** is Lead, Teacher Education and Development at the New South Wales Education and Standards Authority, Australia.

**Graham Hendry** is a Senior Lecturer in the Sydney School of Education and Social Work, The University of Sydney, Australia.

**Maria A. Karimullah** is an academic in the Sydney School of Education and Social Work, The University of Sydney, Australia.

**Anne Lawson-Jones** is a freelance academic based in the United Kingdom.

**Damian Maher** is a Senior Lecturer in Initial Teacher Education at the University of Technology Sydney, Australia.

**Louisa Peralta** is an Associate Professor and Program Director of Health and Physical Education in the Sydney School of Education and Social Work, The University of Sydney, Australia.

**Christine Preston** is an Associate Professor in Primary Science Education in the Sydney School of Education and Social Work, The University of Sydney, Australia.

**Jennifer Rowley** is a Professor Higher Education Practice at the Sydney Conservatorium of Music, The University of Sydney, Australia.

**Alyson Simpson** is a Professor of Education in the Sydney School of Education and Social Work, The University of Sydney, Australia.

**Jim Tognolini** is a Professor and the Director of the Centre for Educational Measurement and Assessment at the University of Sydney, Australia.

**Rachel White** is a Senior Lecturer, Learning Environments and Pedagogy at Western Sydney University, Australia.

# How the book came to be written

So that the evolution of a world-first process for measuring and support-ing teacher quality could be told in its entirety, the WtE team decided to publish a book that drew together all steps of the study as well as its driv-ing rationale. Because the study makes use of cross disciplinary approaches to research and mixed methods, if papers were written instead of chap-ters, they would have been separated out in publication across multiple journals and the overall narrative would have been lost. Instead, the research team took up the challenge to combine forces across theoretical paradigms and work together to write and peer review each other's writ-ing. This has been a collaborative process with all members of the team taking different roles and responsibilities. During the study the research team changed, so not all of the authors worked on the writing to the end of the project. However, where members of the research team contributed to the data analysis process and write up that subsequently became chap-ter content, they are listed as authors.

# Acknowledgements

The What's the Evidence (WtE) team would like to acknowledge past members of the WtE team.

Christine Evans is a highly valued Aboriginal researcher who worked with the WtE team in the first year of the study in addition to her existing commitments. Unfortunately, she did not have capacity to continue beyond that time. While she was with us, she provided expert advice about culturally responsive research design, methods and data analysis.

Two project managers helped to support this study in its beginnings and as it came to a close. Dr Joel Craddock started with the team as a PhD candidate, and is now a Career Development Fellow and Lecturer at the University of Wollongong, Australia. He started with the team back in 2021 and help set up the collaborative and robust research practices that shaped the whole study.

Kathryn Roberts Parker joined the team as a Research Fellow and Project Manager in 2024 to help manage the study to its conclusion. She has been instrumental in managing relationships with stakeholders, supporting team members with written and practical work, and keeping the study on track. Both Joel and Kathryn have made an immense impact on the study and were a fabulous support to the whole team.

We would also like to acknowledge the work of Fang-Tzu (Agnes) Hu, our Research Assistant. Agnes is that rare combination of capable, enthusiastic, and collegial, and always happy to complete any work sent her way, from coding to literature reviewing to referencing. The WtE team is immensely grateful for the high quality support she provided throughout the study.

The study described in this book was funded by the New South Wales Department of Education. The views expressed in this book are the authors' and do not necessarily reflect those of the New South Wales Department of Education.

# Acronyms and abbreviations

| | |
|---|---|
| *AfGT* | Assessment for Graduate Teaching |
| *APST* | Australian Professional Standards for Teachers |
| *ECTs* | Early Career Teachers |
| *ITE* | Initial Teacher Education |
| *TPA* | Teaching Performance Assessment |
| *WtE* | What's the Evidence |

# 1 Understanding teacher quality through a teacher identity lens

*Rachel White, Jennifer Rowley, and Alyson Simpson*

## Introduction

In 2022, the UNESCO Education summit highlighted the role of teachers in transforming education as a key axis point (United Nations, 2022). Teachers have a central role in not only providing high-quality teaching that positively impacts student learning outcomes, but also in promoting emotional support, social development, and student wellbeing (Chetty et al., 2014; Darling-Hammond & Richardson, 2009). This scholarship calls attention to the multifaceted impact teachers can have on students as future social citizens. Global interest in education as a fundamental public good (UNESCO, 2022) recognises the need to revitalise efforts to achieve UNESCO's (2015) sustainable goal number 4, 'to ensure inclusive and equitable quality education and promote lifelong learning opportunities for all'. To accelerate progress on achieving international education goals (United Nations, 2022), teachers, teaching, and the teaching profession have been named under a collective key theme that requires greater action.

Despite the recent global call for action, the status of the teaching profession is in urgent need of further support, as teacher attrition rates continue to rise globally (Amitai & Van Houtte, 2022; García et al., 2022) leading to critical teacher shortages in the United Kingdom (Maisuria et al., 2023), Australia (Australian Government Department of Education, 2022), Europe (Federičová, 2021) and Africa (Kabir, 2023). The pandemic highlighted existing systemic cracks and policy deficits, and placed increased pressure for successful performance on school leaders and administrators (Longmuir, 2023), teachers (Fray et al., 2023) and students (Longmuir et al., 2021), which were further heightened in remote, rural, and regional schools (McPherson et al., 2024). According to a report by the Organization for Economic Co-operation and Development (OECD) in 2021, the disruptive effects of the pandemic and intensification of workloads have exacerbated existing challenges in the teaching profession, leading to increased stress

DOI: 10.4324/9781003542575-1

levels among teachers and higher rates of attrition. Additionally, Harris and Jones (2020) and Mockler (2022) highlight the impacts of negative media reports on the public's perception of teaching, further complicating efforts to recruit and retain educators. Considering these challenges, advocating for teachers and teaching has become a pressing priority, particularly in the political landscape, to ensure the provision of quality education in post-pandemic times.

Globally, governments are directing energy and resources towards policies designed to monitor, shape, and improve the quality, practice, and effectiveness of teachers. Many systems have articulated the knowledge and skills teachers must demonstrate in standards of practice (Darling-Hammond, 2021). This work has been driven by policies attempting to address educational stagnation and declines in student learning, as well as global debates about the limited capacities of schools and teachers to prepare young people for the demands of a rapidly changing world (Flores, 2011, 2016). Grounded in research on effective teaching, these standards articulate what teachers should know and be able to do in clear ways that can guide teachers' preparation, practice, assessment, and professional growth (Darling-Hammond, 2021). The standards make clear the expectations for teachers as well as for those who support them (i.e., teacher educators and school leaders).

Across countries including Canada, the United Kingdom, Australia, and China, professional teaching standards have many commonalities, yet there are also cultural differences. Research focusing on teaching standards (Dinham, 2016; Rizvi & Lingard, 2000; White, 2016) reports that knowledge, primarily pedagogical knowledge, emerges overwhelmingly as the most heavily valued feature of the profession, especially for early career teachers (Goodwin, 2021). Although standards are expected to shape generic as well as specific teacher practices, prompt teacher preparation, and inform selection and accreditation, these standards tend to reduce the complexity of teachers' work to narrowly focus on what teachers know and do. The reduction ignores the teacher who is responsible for doing the teaching. The implicit exclusion of essential teacher qualities such as self-efficacy, resilience, and adaptability, can have potential negative effects on teachers who need professional support to develop these qualities over time (Teng & Alonzo, 2023). A lack of support for the development of teacher quality may lead to burnout and a reduction in effectiveness, as the interpersonal labour of teaching takes a toll on emotional capacity (Connell, 2009). By viewing the profession through the lens of policies and standards, we emphasise and value what we measure—how much a teacher knows and what they do. To respond to the UNESCO call for action we need to find ways to recognise and measure what we value in terms of teacher quality.

**Teacher identity**

To shift the focus from examining teaching practices to exploring teacher quality, we need to consider what it means to be a teacher, including how we define 'teacher' both as an individual and as a social identity.

Identity encompasses various aspects of an individual's self-perception and serves as the foundation for understanding continuity and change in an individual over time. Identities are formed through the exploration and integration of various aspects of one's sense of self, including personal characteristics, roles, and group affiliations. Teacher identity formation can begin when we first interact with teachers as students, identifying what we do and do not like about their conduct through our own educational experiences (Buchanan, 2015). However, it is when an individual chooses to begin their professional training for a teaching career that a more formal engagement with teacher identity development begins (Cooper & Olson, 1996).

During teacher identity formation, individuals may engage in self-reflection, experimentation, and decision making to define their values, beliefs, and goals (Friesen & Besley, 2013). This process often involves exploring different identities, roles, and relationships to establish a sense of continuity and coherence in one's self-concept. The nature of teacher identity has been described as multidimensional, multilayered, dynamic, continuous (Cooper & Olson, 1996), fluid (Akkerman & Meijer, 2011), and in a process of continual restructuring (Karaolis & Philippou, 2019). It can be shaped by personal history, preservice experiences, workplace context (Flores & Day, 2006), and connections with influential others (Morrison, 2013). It can be a complex and ongoing journey as individuals navigate the challenges of self-discovery and self-definition, ensuring identity change and development is both "possible and inevitable" (Burke & Stets, 2023, p. 214). It is best challenged, evaluated and developed through comprehensive reflection on practice by the individual (Buchanan, 2015; Flores & Day, 2006; Friesen & Besley, 2013; Morrison, 2013). Professional or teacher identity formation is a "process through which individuals come to interact and adapt to the expectations of others and the environment" (Day, 2017, p. 159).

According to researchers such as Burke and Stets (2023), Davis et al. (2019), and Stets and Serpe (2013), identities can be understood through three bases: person, role, and group or social. Person identity relates to one's unique self, role identity pertains to the positions one occupies, and group/social identity involves membership in specific communities or social categories. Individuals navigate and express their identities in alignment with each other, guided by their personal identity meanings. An individual's identity is informed by their perception and understanding of the self, their roles, their groups, and their categories. Group or social identity refers to belonging to a particular community, such as a family or political organisation, while social identity denotes one's position within the broader social structure, like race or gender. These two aspects are interconnected and form a unified contextual basis of identity. The self then emerges from, is influenced by, and has influence over the relationships between situated social structures, context, culture, and an individual's relational interactions with others.

The role of a teacher is important to consider when exploring the relationship between teacher identity and teacher quality. While the identity of a teacher is assumed and flexibly defined by the individual, teacher roles can be prescribed by government, and social policy and practice (Martin & Strom, 2016). Public representations of teachers have changed over time creating contrasting identities, for example, the traditional view of teacher as transmitter of knowledge (Cochran-Smith & Fries, 2005; Zeichner, 2005) to the more recent view of teacher as professional knowledge makers (Buchanan, 2015). Policies can also influence how individuals utilise an 'identity standard' – a set of meanings that define the character of an identity (Burke & Stets, 2023) – to process how they perceive the environment and social situations and to inform their emotional, cognitive, and behavioural responses. The meanings that define an identity standard may be determined by personal, social, and cultural influences, and may be consistent for certain role identities, such as 'teacher'. However, how those meanings are dispersed, or their perceived importance for an individual, may vary. This dispersion of meaning can allow for flexibility in how an individual plays out their role in a variety of contexts. Teacher identity standards are constantly being challenged and informed by the behaviours, perceptions, and emotions of situations, which can serve to affirm and/or disavow a person's identity, leaving it in a state of constant change. It also represents an inherent tension in the teaching profession, particularly when individual and contextual understanding of teaching appears in conflict with the shared cultural and political understanding of the teaching profession. This tension, and the concepts we associate with teacher identities, inspired our investigation into teacher quality in a study called *What's the Evidence*.

## What's the Evidence?

*What's the Evidence?: Developing indicators of teacher quality to investigate the predictive validity of teaching performance assessments* (WtE) was a cross-sectoral, multi-year research project investigating potential indicators of teacher quality and the processes by which teacher quality may be measured, by the profession and for the profession. Funded by the New South Wales Department of Education, it was a project incorporating local and international teachers and researchers, as well as educational and systemic leadership perspectives. The study was designed to create a robust construct of teacher quality by forming a solid evidence base from which constant critiques of teacher quality could be addressed. It is the first research-informed attempt to build an evidence base to determine the predictive validity of a teaching performance assessment (TPA) in alignment with indicators of teacher quality. Our focus on creating a research-informed, holistic view of teacher quality has the potential to change how we communicate about teachers and build capacity and confidence in the teaching profession.

### Teacher quality

Despite agreement that teacher quality matters to student achievement, there is "no shared consensus on what factors enhance or even signal" determinants of teacher quality (Harris & Sass, 2011, p. 798). When used, the term is mostly associated with judgements of teaching effectiveness on a cline of value from 'good' to 'poor', or 'high' to 'low'. However, research that refers to this interpretation of the term acknowledges that measurable proxies such as salary, qualifications or experience (García & Weiss, 2019; Hanushek et al., 2005; Strong, 2011; Wiswall, 2013) are used to stand in for quality. The problem with this evidence base, is that it is often difficult to justify as additional factors may be indirectly related to the teachers whose capacity to value-add is being judged. For example, teachers may be assessed on their impact on student outcomes (Fauth et al., 2019; Hanushek & Rivkin, 2006) without consideration of the impact that student-centric and out of school factors such as home environments can have on student learning.

Commentary from the Australian Government Productivity Commission (2022) refers to teacher quality as the cognitive and non-cognitive attributes individual teachers possess, purporting the need for more holistic and comprehensive definitions and measures of teacher quality to be created. Therefore, there is a strong need for educational researchers to identify characteristics that contribute to teacher quality (Biesta et al., 2015; Gilmore & Kramer, 2019; Haddix, 2015). There have been multiple attempts previously to identify individual indicators, with recent research focusing on personal traits and socialisation capabilities (Casely-Hayford et al., 2022; Zavelevsky & Lishchinsky, 2020), resilience (Ainsworth & Oldfield, 2019), cultural responsiveness (Australian Institute for Teaching and School Leadership, 2022), cognitive processing (Bardach & Klassen, 2020), patience (Alzobiani, 2020) and responsibility (Hautz, 2022). Previous studies have recorded the importance of determining core teacher qualities because they have a strong impact on student learning and wellbeing (Rinaldo et al., 2009; Sahin & Adiguzel, 2014). However, there is no common understanding of what constitutes teacher quality holistically (Churchward & Willis, 2019;

Sullivan et al., 2021). Yet, despite the lack of a strong research informed basis on which teacher quality could be judged, education systems have designed measures that only assess teaching performance.

### Teaching performance assessments (TPAs)

The generic term TPA refers to a tool to measure performance at "the intersection of teacher learning, professional practice, and student learning" (Cochran-Smith, 2001, p. 537). Commonly used in the USA, the Performance Assessment of California Teachers (PACT) and the Educative Teacher Performance Assessment (edTPA) were created as multiple measure assessments to meet requirements for employment certification. In other countries TPAs have been designed to authentically evaluate preservice teachers' (PSTs) teaching performance against professional standards as a capstone assessment prior to graduation. International research has positioned TPAs at the start of a continuum of teachers' learning and assessment through their career (Darling-Hammond, 2012). The TPA was introduced in Australia as a solution for addressing key recommendations from a national report into the quality of initial teacher education (ITE) and the preparation of graduating teachers (Craven et al., 2014).

In Australia, the TPA acts not only as a gateway to employment but can also serve as a bridge between ITE and independent professional practice. Rather than mandate a particular approach to TPA design, the Australian Institute for Teaching and School Leadership (AITSL) seed funded two consortia of ITE institutions to devise their own versions. The inclusion of reflective practice is a key element of one TPA, the A*f*GT, which represents teaching as knowledge-informed intellectual work involving professional decisions (Stacey et al., 2019). Thus far, more than 12 models of TPAs have been developed in Australia as tools intended to be robust assessments of classroom readiness. However, currently no evidence base exists to measure the predictive validity of these TPAs, and TPAs have not yet been correlated with indicators of teacher quality as 'fit for purpose' for the profession. This book describes a study that sought to address this challenging tension.

### The WtE research process

Initially, the WtE study intended to delineate a process by which teacher quality could be reconceptualised, measured and supported. To achieve this objective, the research team planned to build and validate a research-informed construct of teacher quality, which could be used to test the predictive validity of one example of a TPA for Australian graduates. The study asked four core, broad research questions:

1   What indicators of teacher quality are identified by stakeholders and the literature as relevant to early career teachers?
2   What valid and reliable evidence needs to be collected to make judgements about these indicators to calculate the predictive validity of a TPA?
3   How do educational stakeholders evaluate the alignment of indicators of teacher quality with early career graduates of the Assessment *for* Graduate Teachers (A*f*GT) in NSW?
4   How well does the AfGT operate as an accurate predictor of teacher quality?

The WtE research aimed to look beyond teaching standards to highlight the contextual, situated, and relational work of teachers and determine if the TPA could predict the future performance of graduates as effective teachers. However, in the process of creating, consulting on, and refining the Teacher Quality Construct based on contemporary indicators (and associated measures), the WtE team realised that the study had the potential to redirect the discourse on teachers, teaching, and improve understanding of the inherent complexities of the education profession. So, the project became more ambitious as the team recognised the impact the work could have by representing the qualities that a teacher may possess as parts of their teacher identity. By shifting the dominant focus away from what teachers know and can do towards the qualities teachers demonstrate the study attends to the aspects missing from current standards and measurements. As a result, the construct at the centre of the evidence-based and evidence-generating WtE research could usefully inform discussions of teacher identity that need to account for the skills, knowledge, attributes and personal characteristics required to fulfil the role of teacher. Ultimately the research will serve to advocate for appreciation of the difficult and specialist work of teachers, provide pathways for professional learning and raise the status of the profession.

### Teacher Quality Construct

As the UNESCO theme suggests the profession needs to think about teaching, and more importantly, teachers, in new ways, by focusing on teachers' willingness to adapt, their capability to communicate and meet challenges, and their overall sense of professionalism. Amongst other influences that are dependent on the individual, teacher quality guides the formation, development, and enactment of teacher identity. It encapsulates characteristics, traits, and attitudes that are malleable, complex, and in flux as teachers move and learn from different relationships with students, colleagues, and families across contexts. The 'identity standard' - the Teacher Quality Construct - was created not to conclusively define the perfect teacher, or to dictate what teachers 'should' be, but to holistically acknowledge the range of qualities teachers may possess and demonstrate in their teaching. The construct is comprised of indicators of teacher qualities - meanings (Burke & Stets, 2023) - that research indicates can be associated with teacher identity. These qualities refer to not only the teaching behaviours or pedagogical strategies that may be observed in a classroom, but also include the qualities that inform the enactment of an individual teacher's identity. The creation and use of the Teacher Quality Construct has formed the basis of our research.

In measurement theory, a construct is "the concept or characteristic that a test is designed to measure" (American Educational Research Association et al., 1999, p. 5). So, the development of a construct is the first stage of creating measures for hard to grasp abstractions. A construct represents a mental perception of an idea, which is informed by a conceptual definition (Braun et al., 2001). At the beginning of the study, as the WtE construct of teacher quality was in its formative stage and no holistic understanding of teacher quality existed, the research team members shared their personal definitions of what the concept of teacher quality meant to them. At the same time a selection of 'grey' literature including policy documentation related to professional standards, teacher accreditation as well as research informed frameworks was searched to establish how education systems defined teacher quality. This review provided an initial set of potential indicators of quality that illuminated our common-sense definition more fully and grounded it in scholarship. The review discovered a tension created between representations of knowledges required for teaching alongside the importance of behavioural attributes and the relational qualities necessary to become a teacher, e.g. "dedication, resilience and passion for the profession" (Paul et al., 2021, p. 11). From this mixture of influences, it became clear to the team that the creation of a research informed evidence base for teacher quality would clarify understanding of a teacher's role as well as enable the profession to more effectively design pathways for teacher growth. Therefore, influenced by our insights as teacher educators, the findings from the grey literature policy search were synthesised and became the initial proxy for the construct of teacher quality that the study would set out to investigate. Figure 1.1 illustrates the original construct for teacher quality proposed by the research team at the commencement of the study.

The WtE team conceptualises the work involved in becoming a teacher as a continuum of connected learning that commences in ITE and continues through teachers' professional engagement in the classroom (Day, 2017) and through professional learning. The Teacher Quality Construct we have adopted for the study refers to a composite of characteristics and attributes, knowledges and intelligences possessed and practiced reflexively by an individual. We identified four components as constitutive of teacher quality: intellectual, interpersonal, affective and intrapersonal.

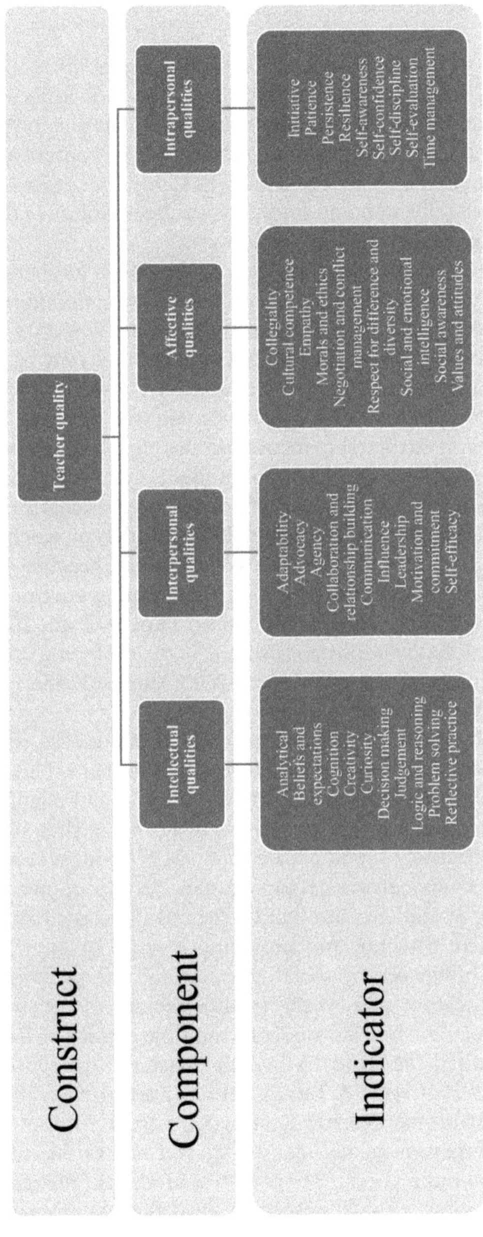



*Figure 1.1* Teacher quality construct initial representation (2021)

A short synthesis of literature expands briefly on each category that also notes their interwoven nature.

1 **Intellectual**: A teacher's cognitive processing abilities (Bardach & Klassen, 2020; Darling-Hammond, 2000). The indicators of quality in this component relate to a teacher's capacity to reason, make informed decisions, and have a professional interest in their content and context. It acknowledges the creative and analytical thinking processes required by teachers to reflect on and interpret practice (Goodwin et al., 2023), which equates to a professional mind-set.

  Evidence of these processes can be found in teachers' planning, gathering of information, judgement, and decision making in efforts to improve student outcomes (Tschannen-Moran & Woolfolk Hoy, 2007). The definition by Alzobiani (2020) supports this view of a teacher's intellectual quality naming it as the capacity "to solve problems, think critically, work collaboratively, and become [sic] effective learner" (p. 33). This area of scholarship focuses on the impact of teachers' beliefs, perceptions and expectations on student learning outcomes and teacher satisfaction as they can affect the way teaching is organised and understood (Muijs & Reynolds, 2002). Studies on teacher thinking report "teachers' mental processes - including teacher beliefs and noticing - have a pervasive effect on the learning environments they create and ultimately, student outcomes" (Roose et al., 2019, p. 141). Studies that note the importance of teachers developing critical thinking or noticing behaviours (Rodgers, 2002; van Es & Sherin, 2002) are common in the literature.

2 **Interpersonal**: The ways in which teachers communicate with, interact with, and understand others, particularly their students. This component acknowledges that teaching is inherently a social and relational profession, and requires teachers to possess dispositions that support their capacity to effectively communicate with others (Donker et al., 2021).

  Research by Knoell et al. (2015) reveals the importance of relationship building to students through teacher qualities such as "a sense of humour, active listening and providing a sense of community" [as] "learning is influenced by social interactions, interpersonal relations, and communication with others" (p. 40). Because of the strong impact of positive relationships on students, multiple studies of teacher effectiveness identify the need to include teachers' interpersonal traits (Alzobiani, 2020; Leggio & Terras, 2019; Marzano et al., 2003; Ziljstra, 2015) as part of the Teacher Quality Construct. Doll et al.'s (2004) work on the creation of resilient classrooms names the capacity for a teacher to maintain good rapport with students as "the most essential ingredient in forging a safe, supportive classroom environment" (p. 18).

  The communicative aspects of educative work are also noted in the literature. Doda and Knowles (2008) list "compassion, respect, personalization, fellowship, and friendship" (p. 27) as characteristics of interactions that will be meaningful to students. More specific identification of communication strengths associated with social interaction such as listening, discerning and interpreting, have been studied by Sahin and Adiguzel (2014) and others. Alzobiani (2020) notes how this quality highlights the "human element in the teaching and learning process" (p. 34). Communication with other stakeholders, such as parents and community members, is key to teachers forming good relationships (Morrison, 2013; Straková et al., 2018).

3  **Affective**: The teacher's capacity to be relatable (Klassen et al., 2018). This component acknowledges the importance of a teacher's attitudes and values in their professional conduct, as well as their sensitivities to the thoughts, feelings, and needs of others. e.g. empathy.

   This component includes multiple ways teachers can understand students' social and educational differences (Pollock & Briscoe, 2019). This can include ethnic, cultural, gender, and class background as well as social position, age, authority, status, occupation, dis/ability, sexual orientation, and place of birth (Banks, 2015; Bonner et al., 2018). In working with students and their peers, it is important that teachers develop an ethical insight and stance. These are fundamental elements of both initial and continuing teacher education as well as ongoing professional learning (Smith, 2014). To support students from different cultural backgrounds, teachers should incorporate prior experience and performance styles of students into teaching design (Boon & Lewthwaite, 2016).
   and

4  **Intrapersonal**: A teacher's ability to take personal responsibility for professional conduct (Klassen et al., 2018; Klassen & Tze, 2014). This component contains indicators related to the way in which a teacher reflects on their personal strengths and weaknesses and how they may impact their behaviour in a professional context.

   In other words, the teacher demonstrates "a sense of internal obligation and commitment to produce or prevent designated outcomes [personal responsibility]" (Lauermann & Karabenick, 2011, p. 127) to "the activity of governing others and the activity of governing oneself [professional conduct]" (Hautz, 2022, p. 213). Sezer et al. (2020) assert that in addition to exhibiting personal responsibility, teachers have an obligation to also demonstrate social and professional responsibility. Alzobiani (2020) identified self-esteem, self-enhancement, and strength of moral character as critical indicators of intrapersonal teacher quality. Time management has also been identified as a key intrapersonal indicator of teacher quality (Bigham et al., 2014; Panayiotou et al., 2014). Effective and efficient time management skills improve both job satisfaction and outcomes (Claessens et al., 2007). Other studies have identified patience (Alzobiani, 2020; Sezer et al., 2020) and self-evaluation (Watson & Beswick, 2011) as important intrapersonal skills.

The chapters that follow in this book tell the story of how the WtE team's initial focus on creating a validation process for an Australian TPA led to the proposition of a new and globally relevant construct for teacher quality. To ensure our construct was fit for purpose to the teaching profession, a robust process of construct validity testing was built into the WtE research design. The team engaged in a variety of research processes to inform, refine, and validate the construct through consultation with international research and Australian education stakeholders, as well as address the research questions.

Chapter 2 details the different methodological and analytical approaches utilised throughout the research process, providing examples of the viable and appropriate methods that can be used when investigating educational phenomena. Chapter 3 describes the scoping review of research published from 2011 – 2021 undertaken by the research team. It focused on seeking current and detailed evidence of how teacher quality is presented in educational research by conducting an evaluation of over 1,000 publications across a 10-year period to begin the validation process of the Teacher Quality Construct.

Chapters 4, 5, and 6 describe different stages of a modified Delphi process that was used to confirm the construct for the early career teacher context. School, industry, and education department leaders as well as schoolteachers across New South Wales, Australia were consulted about their perspectives on the essential qualities of early career teachers, with both qualitative and quantitative methods used to analyse the findings. Chapter 7 introduces a process to develop a scale for measuring teacher quality that could be used to determine the predictive validity of an Australian TPA. Chapter 8 considers the possible international implications of our work by exploring how educators can redirect the discourse about teaching and teachers by focusing on teacher quality.

## Concluding thoughts

The research project described in this book represents a comprehensive exploration of teacher quality. Recognising teachers' adaptability, communication skills, and professionalism is crucial for fostering effective education. The Teacher Quality Construct is not a means to judge the standard or value of a person to the profession. Rather, influenced by a general theory of self that borrows from sociological and psychological models of identity (Davis et al., 2019; Stets & Burke, 2000) it proposes a conceptualisation of teacher quality that accounts for who teachers are as well as what they do. A framing through identity theory allows us to attend not only to the individual, but also to the roles they undertake and the social contexts in which they teach. This provides not just the context of a professional existence but also allows the humanness of the individual to emerge

(Burke & Stets, 2023; Stets & Burke, 2014; Stets & Serpe, 2013). It also helps us understand the importance of providing teachers with processes to authenticate their personal and/or professional identity as effective teachers.

The identity of a teacher is complex; embracing this complexity by investigating teacher quality could help improve understanding of the teaching profession, making it more inclusive and equitable. In identifying the indicators of teacher quality and acknowledging the fluid and multidimensional nature of teacher identity development, the scope for professional learning will be broadened, helping teachers to reflect on their practice, their students, their social context, and how they can continue to develop as professionals. Our research advocates for shifting the discourse towards the intricacies of teachers' attitudes, behaviours, and dispositions supporting more nuanced conversations that account for what it means to be an effective educator and why teachers matter.

## Key References


Churchward, P., & Willis, J. (2019). The pursuit of teacher quality: Identifying some of the multiple discourses of quality that impact the work of teacher educators. *Asia-Pacific Journal of Teacher Education*, *47*(3), 251–264. https://doi.org/10.1080/1359866X.2018.1555792

Darling-Hammond, L. (2021). Defining teaching quality around the world. *European Journal of Teacher Education*, *44*(3), 295–308. https://doi.org/10.1080/02619768.2021.1919080

Fray, L., Jaremus, F., Gore, J., Miller, A., & Harris, J. (2023). Under pressure and overlooked: The impact of COVID-19 on teachers in NSW public schools. *Australian Educational Researcher*, *50*(3), 701–727. https://doi.org/10.1007/s13384-022-00518-3

Friesen, M. D., & Besley, S. C. (2013). Teacher identity development in the first year of teacher education: A developmental and social psychological perspective. *Teaching and Teacher Education*, *36*, 23–32. https://doi.org/10.1016/j.tate.2013.06.005

Mockler, N. (2022). *Constructing teacher identities: How the print media define and represent teachers and their work*. Bloomsbury Publishing. https://doi.org/10.5040/9781350132917

Sahin, A., & Adiguzel, T. (2014). Effective teacher qualities from international mathematics, science, and computer teachers' perspectives. *Eurasia Journal of Mathematics, Science & Technology Education*, *10*(6), 635–646. https://doi.org/10.12973/eurasia.2014.1219a

# 2 A methodological overview of the What's the Evidence study

## Theory and practice

*Maria A. Karimullah, Wayne Cotton, and Louisa Peralta*

### Introduction

The foundation of any robust research project is in its methodology, which plays a fundamental role in the overall research process (Habib et al., 2014). The choice of methodological tools and approaches should closely align with the intent of the research and support its investigation. To support this study with a suitable research framework, it was essential to situate it within an appropriate research paradigm. Guba (1981) advocates for choosing a paradigm that aligns most closely with the phenomenon under investigation. Similarly, Howe and Eisenhart (1990) argue that the chosen methodology should be evaluated based on its alignment with addressing the research questions.

The initial intent of the What's the Evidence (WtE) study was to establish a research informed evidence base for a construct of teacher quality that has never previously been proposed. The translational focus of the WtE study was to then create a validation process for a measurement of teacher quality uniquely suited to the education profession. To meet the twin goals of the research study, a combination of qualitative and quantitative methods and analytic processes was needed. Consequently, a multi-faceted, sequentially stepped, mixed-methods approach was selected. A mixed-methods design avoids reliance solely on either qualitative or quantitative methods and offers a comprehensive understanding of the complex research phenomena investigated in the WtE study.

Qualitative methods are usually associated with understanding personal experiences, behaviours, and insights in a natural environment (Creswell & Creswell, 2017). Rather than quantifying information, the goal of qualitative methods is to thoroughly examine and explain experiential data and therefore the method suits the conceptualisation of an evidence-informed construct through meaning making exercises. By prioritising a comprehensive analysis and interpretation of empirical data, this approach aligns well with the idea of fostering the creation of a

DOI: 10.4324/9781003542575-2

Teacher Quality Construct based on research evidence extracted from meaningful exploration of concepts in interaction with stakeholders.

Quantitative methods are generally research approaches that rely on numerical data and statistical analysis. They are often applied to test, measure, and quantify theories (Creswell & Creswell, 2017). They are closely associated with modern assessment theories. Unlike qualitative methods, which focus on understanding subjective experiences, quantitative methods aim to provide objective and generalisable findings. Therefore, the quantitative approach was needed for both the construct validation process, as well as for the standard setting exercises undertaken during the creation of measurement scales.

Confirming the importance of methodological stand points, the choice of mixed methods for this study has impacted directly on the language used to represent both processes and outcomes. For example, in early presentations the WtE team adopted terms that aligned closely with qualitative research to explain the emerging conceptualisation of the Teacher Quality Construct. Therefore, the indicators making up the construct were initially coded into four *categories* to group associated, similar concepts. Given the use of the Delphi process, the term *domains* could have been chosen to signify the difference in indicator groupings from a qualitative perspective. However, as the study progressed, the focus on the creation of scales for use with the Teacher Quality Construct required a change of terminology to achieve methodological consistency with modern measurement theory. Therefore, the Teacher Quality Construct is now referred to as having four *components* with multiple indicators, as this representation allows for measurement of indicator presence by amount rather than just by appropriateness.

These deliberations demonstrate that by integrating the strengths of both methodological approaches, researchers can obtain a clear vision of the intricate dynamics of a problem. Creswell and Creswell (2017) posits that mixed-methods research can be implemented in a sequential manner, either commencing with qualitative data collection followed by quantitative analysis, or vice versa. For instance, a researcher might initially conduct a quantitative survey to identify important variables related to a particular research problem. They might then perform qualitative interviews as an additional method to learn more about the significance and experiences of individuals within that context. This allows a holistic understanding that includes both rich, in-depth insights and generalisable conclusions. Another strategy is to establish hypotheses using quantitative data, followed by qualitative research to further investigate these ideas. A more thorough comprehension of the research topic and related contextual influences may result from this iterative process, which was the intention of the mixed-methods approach to the WtE research study.

This chapter introduces the key methods and analytic processes that have been used throughout the What's the Evidence (WtE) study. The WtE project was a complex, mixed-methods four-year research study conducted to build and test a new construct of teacher quality. To systematically address the complex set of research questions that the WtE team were addressing, the study was conducted in a series of interrelated steps, each building on the outcomes of the previous step/s. This structured approach enabled the research to progress logically and cohesively, with each step contributing to the overall goal of developing a robust construct of teacher quality and a process for measuring the predictive validity of TPAs.

The study asked the following research questions:

1  What indicators of teacher quality are identified by stakeholders and the literature as relevant to early career teachers?
2  What valid and reliable evidence needs to be collected to make judgements about these indicators to calculate the predictive validity for a TPA?
3  How do stakeholders evaluate the alignment of indicators of teacher quality with early career graduates of the Assessment for Graduate Teaching (A*f*GT) in NSW?
4  How well does the A*f*GT operate as an accurate predictor of teacher quality?

The study was structured with three phases. In 2021, the first phase of the project commenced with the proposition of a Teacher Quality Construct informed by key indicators collected from grey literature. A scoping review of academic literature was then used to establish a scholarly, research informed evidence base for the Teacher Quality Construct. Through the second phase in 2022, the researchers tested the construct for fit for purpose use with early career teachers by adopting a modified Delphi process to generate conceptual consensus across disparate groups of stakeholders. Focus groups and surveys were adopted in phase two to collect qualitative and quantitative data supporting the exploratory nature of the study. The survey data from this phase were analysed using Classical Test Theory (CTT) including Confirmatory Factor Analysis (CFA) and Rasch Theory (RT). The third and final phase commenced in 2023 and focused on testing a sample of indicators by adopting measurement tools confirmed as valid in the scoping review process. Discussion and survey tools also informed the standard setting exercises undertaken with groups of teachers and school leaders. Data collected from these participants were analysed using modern measurement theory tools as part of a detailed research design process, aiming to test the predictive validity of a TPA against the research informed construct of teacher quality.

The next section of the chapter introduces the study's four main methodological tools in the order they were adopted for the study. The methods are first explained in relation to their use in general educational research. Then, an application of each method in the context of this study is provided including a rationale for its suitability to the research question being addressed in that phase of the study.

### Scoping review

Although there is no single, authoritative definition of a scoping review, it will generally involve one or more elements, such as literature mapping, conceptual mapping, and policy mapping (Anderson et al., 2008). Despite being a relatively new method for exploring the literature (Davis et al., 2009), scoping reviews are increasingly popular for synthesising research evidence in fields such as education, human resource planning, and allied health (Daudt et al., 2013; Davis et al., 2009; Levac et al., 2010). Researchers have suggested that scoping reviews will be useful for rapidly mapping significant ideas within a research area (Mays et al., 2005). They are expected to be a rigorous technique for identifying primary and secondary sources of literature, with success contingent upon both progressive and academic approaches (Davis et al., 2009). As Davis et al. (2009) argue, scoping reviews will provide insight into the 'what' and 'why of a research area, offering a comprehensive overview that goes beyond merely identifying 'who', 'where', and 'how'.

Scoping reviews are particularly valuable when a research area has not been extensively or comprehensively reviewed, or when the topic is complex or heterogeneous in nature (Pham et al., 2014). When comparing scoping reviews with systematic reviews, the former are frequently utilised in areas where high-quality evidence may be limited. This allows for inclusion of a broader range of research designs and potentially incorporating literature that might not be considered in a more rigorous systematic review (Levac et al., 2010). In contrast, systematic reviews are typically employed to answer specific questions, with stringent methods for evaluating the quality of articles (O'Brien et al., 2010). A scoping review is more appropriate for identifying, mapping, and examining key characteristics within the literature (Larsen et al., 2019; Munn et al., 2018).

The scoping review of contemporary educational research aimed to contribute to the field through investigation into valid and reliable studies from around the world that have sought to identify indicators of teacher quality. Publications from a global search were included in the review, reflecting the constantly evolving policies affecting the teaching profession and initial teacher education worldwide (Bahadir & Tuncer, 2020; Darling-Hammond, 2012; Ingvarson & Rowe, 2008). The approach taken in this review was aligned with the WtE research study, drawing conclusions from existing literature on teacher quality, to build and refine a construct. As the evidence-informed construct was the first attempt at bringing expansive and diverse research literature together, the scoping review method was the most appropriate choice.

Information collected through the scoping review also provided an opportunity for the WtE team to identify the measurement instruments employed in previous studies of teacher quality. The research team carefully reviewed the included studies for evidence of validity confirmation. This process generated a comprehensive list of tools, some of which were adopted for use within the WtE research study.

## The Delphi and modified Delphi methods

The Delphi method is a structured communication process involving procedures designed to create consensus (Green, 2014). It is frequently utilised to collect expert opinions on real-world issues (Naisola-Ruiter, 2022). Founded in the 1950s by researchers Dalkey and Helmer at the RAND Corporation (Dalkey & Helmer, 1963), it is a research method that entails use of an iterative rounds of questionnaires or interviews with a group of specialists, who present their perceptions of a specific topic (Barrios et al., 2021). The results emerging from these multiple rounds of data collection are analysed and synthesised to present the shared opinion of the group and reduce the impact of individual biases. Fletcher and Marchildon (2014, p. 3) state, "the key purpose for using the Delphi method is the collection of a range of informed judgments on issues that are largely unexplored, difficult to define, highly context and expertise specific, or future-oriented".

Over time, the Delphi method has evolved with a variety of modifications. The modified Delphi method is a variation of the traditional Delphi method, designed to enhance its efficiency and applicability in various research contexts, including education (Custer et al., 1999). This method includes modifications such as fewer rounds, structured feedback, and occasionally initial rounds to generate key ideas amongst participants prior to collection of data. Traditionally, the Delphi method leverages anonymity so that participants do not know the identity of others participating in the process (Taylor, 2020). However, there may be occasions when the condition of anonymity is waived to enable a group of participants to meet to air conceptual disagreements (von der Gracht, 2012). This modification to the Delphi process can serve as an opportunity for researchers to gain insights to the reasons why participants agree or disagree with the conceptualisations other panellists support (von der Gracht, 2012). That is, the modified Delphi method may include direct consultation with stakeholders as an initial step prior to surveys of a broader study population (Avella, 2016).

The Delphi method is widely employed in educational contexts to create policies, benchmarks, forecasts regarding new trends, remodelling curricula, and learning experiences to train students for future careers (Green, 2014). Prior to the 1990s, the Delphi method's time-consuming and labour-intensive nature limited its use within the educational field (Weingand, 1998). However, with the growth of digital applications and electronic survey tools in recent times, the process has become efficient, leading to increased adoption among various disciplines including business (Jiang et al., 2017), psychology (Van der Vaart et al., 2014), medicine (Sinha et al., 2011), and education (Zawacki-Richter, 2009). The modified Delphi method has been adopted in the context of teacher education as a valuable tool to develop teaching skills for school teachers (Alake-Tuenter et al., 2013), to define the qualities required for teacher educators (Koster et al., 2005), and to explore the integration of technology into teacher training programs (Volman, 2005).

The modified Delphi method has been beneficial in educational research in establishing guidelines and standards, and in analysing trends (Green, 2014). Hence, for the WtE study a modified Delphi process was deemed relevant as the intent was to gain insights from multiple stakeholder views in the education system. Given the disparate views that exist in the field and the need to create a list of indicators that is relevant to the local context, the modified Delphi method was chosen as the second phase of the WtE study. Two iterative rounds of data collection were run, which collected and synthesised opinions from industry experts, professional association leaders, school leaders and classroom teachers. This process, with the assistance of focus groups, surveys, thematic and statistical analysis using modern measurement theory, helped to test and stabilise our construct of teacher quality.


### *Focus group discussions*

Focus group discussions are one of the most popular research tools in the field of social sciences (Kellmereit, 2015), particularly education (Prosina et al., 2024) and health research (Bennett et al., 2019). A focus group is defined as a group of people selected by investigators to participate in structured, online or face-to-face discussions to explore a research element based on personal perceptions and experience (Almujlli et al., 2022; Galavi & Khajouei, 2023; Kellmereit, 2015). This method includes guided discussions among small groups of participants typically ranging between four to twelve individuals. Focus group analysis attends to what participants say as well as exploring the engagement dynamics within the focus group, specifically how the individuals interact with each other and the process of putting together their contributions (Duggleby, 2005; Leavy, 2007). There are several benefits of focus groups, including that they show

how people's attitudes and thoughts grow and transform, they let participants communicate spontaneously, they allow participants to gain a sense of security, comfort, and confidence, and they allow individuals to feel empowered because of the group setting (Sim, 1998). Moreover, focus groups allow participants to build on each other's concepts and insights during the data collection process (Wire, 2022). This can be very useful in education research because participants may have common perspectives or experiences that can enhance the data collection process.

Based on the findings of research in education, the primary benefit of focus groups is their capacity to allow for a range of opinions and emotional responses to emerge in a group dynamic, which offers shared understanding of the chosen topic or subject. In contrast to other research methods such as one-on-one interviews or in-person observations, focus groups can guarantee more effective information collection in less time (Prosina et al., 2024). However, while focus groups offer the benefit of efficient data collection, they are susceptible to the constraints of self-reporting. Participants may be influenced by social desirability bias, guiding them to deliver answers they consider will be well-received by other participants of the group. Furthermore, the dominating voices in the focus group may overshadow quieter members, therefore affecting the results. To minimise these problems, researchers may collect contrasting data via surveys and/or questionnaires.

The WtE study utilised focus groups because of their long-standing acceptance (Gilflores & Alonso, 1995), 'heuristic value' (Acocella, 2012), and the opportunities presented for participants and researchers to build connection through sharing experiences. To obtain diverse viewpoints and promote consensus among stakeholders at the very start of the study, focus group discussions with an expert panel were integrated into the modified Delphi process. The expert panel served as an advisory consultative group, discovering what these participants thought about the Teacher Quality Construct before the WtE survey tool was widely adopted. Later in the study, focus groups were also adopted as part of the standard setting exercise in phase three where the meetings provided rich opportunities for participants to discuss their perceptions of indicators of self-reflection as a measure of teacher quality. In all, the focus group discussions provided a platform for participants to engage in dialogue, share their insights, jointly explore the professional fit for purpose of the Teacher Quality Construct, and its implications for practice.

### *Surveys*

Survey research is defined as "the collection of information from a sample of individuals through their responses to questions" (Check & Schutt, 2011, p. 160). There are rigorous guidelines for survey methods that have been created to provide results that are reliable, accurate, and valuable. Researchers have provided advice on this topic including the need for developing clear research question/s, carefully planning and piloting survey questions and layout, informing survey respondents of the purpose and rationale behind the survey, providing clear statements to the respondents of incentives that can or cannot be expected, protecting the identity of survey participants, and preparing survey forms in the language of the potential participants (Goodfellow, 2023; Kelley et al., 2003; McNamara, 1993; Phillips et al., 2014; Rea & Parker, 2014). In addition to being a useful tool for descriptive research, surveys may also be used to investigate specific aspects of a situation, search for explanations, and test hypotheses (Kelley et al., 2003).

Survey data may now be created quickly and in large quantities - thanks to automated survey software on internet platforms, as well as the use of email and social media to reach respondents (Ball, 2019). Online surveys are becoming increasingly common in educational research (Park et al., 2019; Roberts & Allen, 2015) because they are perceived to be simple to conduct, tend to have greater response rates, and require fewer resources (in terms of data processing and publication) when compared with paper surveys (Harlow, 2010; Roberts & Allen, 2012). Online surveys have been used to provide valuable insight on a variety of educational topics as diverse as professional learning of higher education teachers (Knight et al., 2006), effective modes of teaching (Evans, 2008), and student rating scales to evaluate teaching (Berk, 2012). The WtE study utilised surveys because of the known benefits including maintenance of participant anonymity, efficiency of recruitment, and response rate (Van Selm & Jankowski, 2006).

All surveys used in WtE were hosted on the Qualtrics platform. A survey that listed indicators from the Teacher Quality Construct was used to collect and synthesise data during the two rounds of the Delphi process from teachers, professional association leads, and the members of the expert panel of stakeholders. Surveys were also used to collect data from teachers and principals/executive teachers in the standard setting exercises and data alignment processes trialled to test the predictive validity of a TPA. These surveys were designed to align with the indicators rated by stakeholders as of particular importance to ECTs and made use of previously validated instruments. The indicators tested in the first trial of a new process to test the predictive validity of a TPA included motivation and commitment, respect for diversity, and reflective practice. For ease of use, the second survey was shorter, and the trial focussed only on items from the reflective practice tool.

The last section of this chapter provides an overview of the primary analytical processes used in the study. First, each form of analysis is explained in the context of its general application to educational research.

Then, each analytic process is discussed in relation to its specific application within this study.

## Thematic analysis

Thematic analysis is a widely used qualitative research method for systematically identifying, organizing, and interpreting patterns of meaning (or themes) within a dataset (Braun & Clarke, 2022). It provides a flexible yet rigorous approach to analysing qualitative data, making it suitable for a variety of research contexts.

Thematic analysis is used in educational research to uncover and interpret the underlying patterns in qualitative data, such as focus group discussions, allowing researchers to better understand the experiences, perceptions, and perspectives of participants (Nowell et al., 2017). This method enables researchers to explore complex educational phenomena by grouping data into themes that provide insights into key issues and relationships relevant to the research questions.

The WtE study employed tailored versions of thematic analysis to systematically explore and identify themes within the data collected during the scoping review, surveys and the focus group discussions.

## Confirmatory Factor Analysis

Confirmatory Factor Analysis (CFA) is pervasive in the social sciences because it addresses theoretical models where the construct is difficult to measure. CFA is "a fundamental method for evaluating the internal structural validity of measurement instruments" (Rogers, 2024, p. 6634), which therefore can be used to assess the 'fit' of items being proposed as effectively representing the underlying construct. Central to the work of CFA is the examination of structural relationships among entities that seem disparate but may belong within a complex model. One of the benefits of CFA is that it enables ongoing validation as understanding of a construct evolves (Rogers, 2024).

CFA is used in education research when instrumentation is needed to quantify phenomena that are not directly observable, e.g. student knowledge (Reeves & Marbach-Ad, 2016). Research related to learning and understanding has made use of CFA for program evaluation and assessment purposes (e.g. Denofrio et al., 2007; Smith et al., 2013). The types of instrumentation yielding quantitative data suitable for CFA analysis include survey, questionnaire and self-report (e.g. belief scales) that contain Likert-type items, each with multiple response alternatives.

The WtE study used CFA because, while the construct was based on a sound theoretical conception of teacher quality, and was put through external content review, the team also needed to explicitly report an evidence-based validity argument for the Teacher Quality Construct.

## Rasch modelling

The Rasch model is a psychometric framework used for analysing categorical data, such as responses to questionnaires or test items (Biçer & Batdı, 2019; Frye et al., 2024; Girgin, 2020). In other words, it is a model used to measure underlying constructs that cannot be directly noticed, such as attitudes, personality traits, or intelligence. Rasch modelling is an invaluable instrument in education research, which aids the identification of misfitting items in measurements thereby improving the validity, reliability and accuracy of educational assessments.

Research in various educational contexts, including physics education and teacher evaluation, has successfully employed Rasch modelling to enhance assessment instruments, showcasing its flexibility and effectiveness in strengthening educational research results (Bailes & Nandakumar, 2020; Van Zile-Tamsen, 2017). For example, Rasch modelling was utilised in a study by Van Zile-Tamsen (2017) to create a rating scale for teacher responses, confirming the validity and reliability of the scale. Planinic et al. (2019) enhanced the construct and assessment of diagnostic instruments in physics education by employing Rasch analysis, which improved the tracking of students' learning progress. Rasch modelling was also utilised by Bailes and Nandakumar (2020) to improve the survey tools that education leaders use, leading to more reliable and successful data collection.

Both CFA and Rasch modelling were used in this research to interrogate the results of the iterative survey rounds to measure how well indicators fit the Teacher Quality Construct. The methods were utilised to obtain a detailed item analysis that allows the researchers to ensure the reliability and validity of the construct and to gauge the measurement characteristics of rating scales. Statistical verification of the construct validity confirmed that the construct was suitable for adoption in the WtE project context.

While Rasch modelling was used predominantly to help develop the Teacher Quality Construct, it was also used to examine the unidimensionality of the indicators identified through the modified Delphi process as part of the process to create a scale of teacher quality to investigate the predictive validity of the A*f*GT TPA.


## Conclusion

This chapter has provided a detailed rationale of the methods adopted in the WtE study. The selection of methods was guided by the specific research questions and the overall objectives of the study, ensuring that each method contributes effectively to the investigation. The chapter provides a theoretical grounding that underscores the study's aim to develop a novel construct of teacher quality through a complex and scholarly investigation of components and indicators and test its use in the creation of a process to assess the predictive validity of TPAs. A mixed methods approach was adopted, integrating a scoping review of literature, a modified Delphi process, and a standard setting exercise. The mixed methods approach was particularly beneficial, as it allowed for a greater depth and breadth of information than would be possible using a single method alone (Almalki, 2016).

The research was designed to move from creation of a proposed construct of teacher quality, which informed the foundational elements of the study, and progressed to the implementation of advanced quantitative methods to both validate and test the construct. The standard setting exercise validated the quality of the framework's components. Each step in the process is methodologically justified within the context of the research objectives, ensuring that the chosen methods were not only appropriate but also strategically aligned with the overall research design. The utilisation of these methods strengthened the rigor and reliability of the research. By combining these methodological tools, a more comprehensive and nuanced understanding of teacher quality has been achieved. The ethical considerations guaranteed that each method was conducted in coherence with the highest standards of fair practice. Together, these methods allowed for a comprehensive and rigorous research process.

In conclusion, the methodological approach employed in the WtE study provides a robust foundation for the subsequent analysis and findings presented in the following chapters. The utilisation of specific methods and adherence to ethical principles enhance the credibility and validity of the research, particularly in exploring key themes such as teacher quality, teacher identity, and the development and evaluation of early career teachers. This foundation sets the stage for the detailed descriptions of each phase in the chapters that follow, offering a deeper exploration of how these methods contributed to the overall purpose of the WtE study.

## Key References

Almalki, S. (2016). Integrating quantitative and qualitative data in mixed methods research – Challenges and benefits. *Journal of Education and Learning, 5*(3), 288–296. https://doi.org/10.5539/jel.v5n3p288

Creswell, J. W., & Creswell, J. D. (2017). *Research design: Qualitative, quantitative, and mixed methods approaches* (4th ed.). Sage.

Daudt, H. M., Van Mossel, C., & Scott, S. J. (2013). Enhancing the scoping study methodology: A large, inter-professional team's experience with Arksey and O'Malley's framework. *BMC Medical Research Methodology, 13*, Article 48. https://doi.org/10.1186/1471-2288-13-48

Gibbons, A. S., & Bunderson, C. V. (2004). Explore, explain, design. In K. Kempf-Leonard (Ed.) *Encyclopedia of social measurement* (Vol. 1, pp. 927–938). https://doi.org/10.1016/B0-12-369398-5/00017-7

Habib, M., Pathik, B. B., & Maryam, H. (2014). *Research methodology - contemporary practices: Guidelines for academic researchers*. Cambridge Scholars Publishing.

Howe, K., & Eisenhart, M. (1990). Standards for qualitative (and quantitative) research: A prolegomenon. *Educational Researcher, 19*(4), 2–9. https://doi.org/10.3102/0013189X019004002

von der Gracht, H. A. (2012b). Consensus measurement in Delphi studies: Review and implications for future quality assurance. *Technological Forecasting and Social Change, 79*(8), 1525–1536. https://doi.org/10.1016/j.techfore.2012.04.013

# 3 Building understanding of teacher quality

## A scoping review

*Wayne Cotton, Louisa Peralta, Alyson Simpson, Rachel White, George Harb, Nicole Hart, Graham Hendry, Maria A. Karimullah, Anne Lawson-Jones, Damian Maher, Christine Preston, Jennifer Rowley, and Jim Tognolini*

## 1 Introduction

It has long been agreed that the provision of high-quality education is imperative to attain the goal of raising the quality of learning for all students, irrespective of characteristics, backgrounds, and locations (Organisation for Economic Co-operation and Development, 2001, 2005). As teachers are recognised as the most valuable resource available to both schools and higher education institutions to enhance students' learning outcomes (Chetty et al., 2014; Hanushek & Rivkin, 2006), an investment in broad ranging teacher qualities and ongoing professionalism is vital. However, the teacher quality most valued in international research on professional standards is teacher knowledge (Dinham, 2016; Rizvi & Lingard, 2000; White, 2016). This content driven judgement is seen to be particularly relevant to early career teachers (Goodwin, 2021). A critical reading of the standards that shape teacher preparation, inform selection and accreditation argues that they do not represent a comprehensive view of teachers' work. That is, the standards tend to reduce the complexity of teachers' work ignoring the teacher who does the teaching. To provide ongoing support for teachers that meets their professional needs over time, consideration of teacher qualities is strongly recommended (Teng & Alonzo, 2023).

This scoping review builds on recent and earlier work of other researchers (Bahadir & Tuncer, 2020; Bardach & Klassen, 2020; Clinton et al., 2018; Hopkins & Stern, 1996; Klassen & Tze, 2014; Roorda et al., 2011), which have emphasised the need to move beyond the focus on quality teaching to a focus on the identification of individual indicators of teacher quality.

DOI: 10.4324/9781003542575-3

As an extensive scoping review of literature focusing exclusively on indicators of teacher quality has not been attempted previously, nor has a scoping review been used to build evidence to support or refine a construct of teacher quality that brings disparate indicators together, this review is original and timely. In addition, this review is highly valuable to Initial Teacher Education (ITE), the profession and ongoing teacher learning and education, as it addresses critical gaps in current discussions of teacher quality. By identifying the research informed indicators of teacher quality, our study can support teacher educators around the world to improve the validity of teacher assessment models at a time when teachers and teacher education are consistently under critique (Simpson et al., 2021). The research informed indicators of teacher quality can also be used to help validate the Teacher Quality Construct outlined in Chapter 1.

### *1.1 Research questions*

The objective of this phase of the What's the Evidence (WtE) study was to focus on the first of the study's overarching research questions: What indicators of teacher quality are identified by stakeholders and the literature as relevant to early career teachers? In order to identify indicators of teacher quality in relevant literature, it was determined that a scoping review of research from the last decade would allow the research team to map evidence of teacher quality in educational literature, and identify "main concepts, theories, sources, and knowledge gaps" (Tricco et al., 2018, p.5) in this area.

## 2  Methods

This phase of the WtE study focused on investigation of indicators of teacher quality in recent literature. As described in Chapter 1, at the commencement of the study the research team created a list of indicators of teacher quality (attributes, dispositions, and behaviours) required for people undertaking teacher roles in education. Initially extracted from a desk review of recent grey literature and policy documents the indicators were collated by semantic association into groups. After discussion informed by the research team's experience in education, these indicators were mapped into four components that formed a proposed Teacher Quality Construct. In order to establish an evidence base for the construct, the WtE team then conducted a rigorous scoping review to systematically explore the expansive and diverse research in the focus area (Armstrong et al., 2011). A scoping review was deemed appropriate because the method provides "a process of retrospectively mapping the existing literature" (Dille & Røkenes, 2021, p. 2), particularly the literature that has not yet been extensively reviewed

(Grant & Booth, 2009). Scoping reviews are also 'an increasingly common approach to informing decision making and research based on the identification and examination of the literature on a given topic' (Peters et al., 2020, p. 2119).

## 2.1 Protocol

This review and subsequent manuscript were designed and written using the PRISMA extension for Scoping Reviews (PRISMA-ScR) (Tricco et al., 2018). The review was registered prospectively with the Open Science Framework on the 23rd of March 2022. The chapter maps closely to the PRISMA protocol overall, however, word limitations preclude provision of more detailed explanation of the optional step of critical appraisal.

## 2.2 Eligibility criteria

The broader research study focused on investigating indicators of quality of teachers involved in formal schooling and educational institutions around the world – in classrooms, administration, and executive leadership. As such, for a publication to be considered eligible for this study, it needed to focus on identifying or describing indicators of teacher quality in teachers working in schools, also known as in-service teachers. The publication also needed to relate to elementary (primary) and/or secondary school teachers only.

## 2.3 Information sources

To find relevant literature a search was conducted using the following electronic databases: A+ Education, Education Source, ERIC, ProQuest Education, PsycINFO, and SAGE Education. These databases were selected as they have a strong focus on peer-reviewed, global educational research. The search strategies were explored, tested, and refined by the two lead researchers, before being executed by the lead researcher in October, 2021. The results were exported into Endnote 20 (Clarivate Analytics), then subsequently imported into Covidence (Clarivate Analytics), an online application designed to manage systematic and scoping reviews of literature.

## 2.4 Search strategy

The search strategy included the use of terms in three broad categories: (i) Population (i.e., teachers); (ii) Concept (i.e., indicators and quality); and (iii) Context (i.e., primary, and secondary schools). As the review focused

*Table 3.1* Search terms used when searching the electronic databases

| Search category | Specific search terms |
| --- | --- |
| Population | teacher* |
| AND | |
| Concept (i.e., indicators) | indicator* OR qualit* OR abilit* OR skill* OR attribute* OR character* OR trait* OR competencies OR feature* OR properties OR aspects OR elements OR facets OR mannerisms OR habits OR customs |
| AND | |
| Context | school* |
| AND | |
| Concept (i.e., quality) | qualit* OR abilit* OR perform* OR achievement OR effective* OR skilled OR skilful OR success* OR competent* OR excel* OR exceptional* OR outstanding OR superior OR advanced |
| AND | |
| Study Type | 'evidence-based' OR effective* OR treatment* OR intervention* OR outcome* OR 'experimental stud*' OR 'quasi-experiment*' OR 'case stud*' OR 'case-control stud*' OR 'cross-sectional' OR 'cohort stud*' OR observational OR 'promising practice*' OR 'randomised control trial*' OR interview* OR 'focus group*' OR narrative* OR qualitative OR survey OR 'pre-experiment*' OR evaluation OR perspective* OR voice* OR experience* OR 'grounded theory' |

on research-based studies, a fourth category (iv) Study type (e.g., randomised control trial) was included. The search terms utilised for the scoping review are presented in Table 3.1.

The search was limited to full text, peer reviewed, academic journal publications written in English and published between 2011 to June 2021. During this period there was an increased emphasis on standards for teacher accreditation (Australian Institute for Teaching and School Leadership, 2011; UK Government Department for Education, 2011) leading to changes in program delivery, teacher education and teacher practices. Additional relevant publications were also identified by hand searching the references in initial publications found in the database search.

### 2.5 Selection of sources of evidence

Covidence was used as the online application to support the selection of sources of evidence in this scoping review that was completed in two stages. In the first stage, 11 researchers individually scanned the titles and abstracts of publications identified in the search to assess if they focused on research informed variables (i.e., indicators) of teacher quality in elementary (primary) or high schools. Publications were excluded if they did not meet these criteria – for example, if the title or abstract indicated the publication focused on teachers in early childhood or pre-school contexts. In the second stage, the same 11 researchers reviewed the remaining full text publications to assess their relevance for inclusion. To increase consistency within the decision making process, three one-hour moderation meetings were conducted. If any of the researchers were unsure of the status of a certain publication, they consulted with the other researchers until a consensus was reached.

## 2.6  Data charting

Data charting is the process through which relevant data are identified, selected and presented in a standardised manner, for example, in a table including frequency counts and/or qualitative content analysis. The specific details of which data to extract were developed through consultation between the lead researchers. Data charting was conducted in Covidence, with 11 researchers independently extracting the data. Each publication was examined by two researchers – one to extract the data and another to confirm or adjust extracted data. To assist with consistency in this process, further moderation meetings were held. Where clarification was needed, researchers consulted with the lead researcher until a consensus was reached.

## 2.7  Data items

The following data were collected from the included publications: author(s), year of publication, origin/country of origin where the study was published or conducted, study population and sample size, methodology, and key findings that related to the study's objectives i.e., reported variables that described the attitudes, dispositions, knowledges, and/or skills of the teacher or teachers under investigation.

## 2.8  Critical appraisal of individual sources of evidence

To align with the objectives of the scoping review, the study types of the individual publications, and the number of included publications, a broad method of critically appraising the sources of evidence was necessary. We chose to evaluate the validity of measures for indicators of teacher quality in a substantial proportion (>70%) of the included publications by assessing whether the authors commented on the validity of their research processes. Validating a selected subset of publications allowed for a more thorough and manageable analysis within the available resources, ensuring the feasibility and effectiveness of the validation efforts. Furthermore, to enhance the reliability of the process, each publication was appraised twice, and inter-rater reliability was assessed using percentage agreement.

## 2.9 Synthesis of results

To synthesise the results, this scoping review utilised the Teacher Quality Construct presented in Chapter 1, a composite of characteristics and attributes, knowledges and intelligences possessed and practiced reflexively by an individual. This construct encapsulates the multifaceted nature of a teacher's work. It adopts a holistic perspective, recognising the complex interplay of various teacher attributes and competencies, and emphasises that teacher quality extends beyond mere content delivery. The construct draws on cognitive processing abilities (Bardach & Klassen, 2020; Darling-Hammond, 2000), relationship building abilities (Grönqvist & Vlachos, 2016), the capacity to relate to others and be relatable (Klassen et al., 2018), and the ability to take personal responsibility for professional conduct (Klassen et al., 2018; Klassen & Tze, 2014).

Employing the qualitative content analysis method outlined by Drisko and Maschi (2015), the Teacher Quality Construct, including the four components (Intellectual, Interpersonal, Affective, and Intrapersonal) and 37 indicators served as the lens through which the included studies were analysed and synthesised. This approach facilitates an iterative process of category refinement, ensuring a comprehensive and aligned synthesis with the proposed construct. Through this analytical method, it is possible to make "systematic, credible, valid, and replicable inferences" about the presence of teacher quality indicators in the literature (Drisko & Maschi, 2015, p. 8).

Initially, publications were divided based on author surnames into three distinct groups: A–G, H–O, and P–Z. Each group was assigned to a specific team member for detailed coding, with the A–G group serving as a pilot to refine the coding protocol before extending it to the rest of the data.

Data cleaning (Chu et al., 2016; White et al., 2012) was a prerequisite step due to the format in which Covidence presented the extracted information; typically, multiple data points from a single publication were concatenated within a single cell, delineated by commas. For instance, as shown in Table 3.2, manuscript #4119 from Covidence contained four distinct data points within one cell. The team disaggregated these data points, allocating each to a separate row, thereby facilitating a more structured analysis.

The initial coding of the A – G surname group led to the creation of a codebook, designed to ensure consistency and clarity across the coding

*Table 3.2* An example of how the extracted data from a publication were separated into different rows

| Covidence # | Study ID | Title | Extracted data |
|---|---|---|---|
| 4119 | Brix 2014 | Investigating Mandatory Peer Review of Teaching in Schools | Peer review, analysis of student achievement, student feedback mechanisms and personal reflection, professionalism and managerialism. |

…was transformed to…

| Covidence # | Study ID | Title | Extracted data |
|---|---|---|---|
| 4119 | Brix 2014 | Investigating Mandatory Peer Review of Teaching in Schools | Peer review |
| 4119 | Brix 2014 | Investigating Mandatory Peer Review of Teaching in Schools | Analysis of student achievement |
| 4119 | Brix 2014 | Investigating Mandatory Peer Review of Teaching in Schools | Student feedback mechanisms and personal reflection |
| 4119 | Brix 2014 | Investigating Mandatory Peer Review of Teaching in Schools | Professionalism and managerialism. |

*Table 3.3* Sample of extracted data key words to help guide the coding process

| Component | Indicator | Data key words |
|---|---|---|
| 1. Intellectual qualities | Beliefs and expectations | Beliefs |
| 1. Intellectual qualities | Beliefs and expectations | Believing |
| 1. Intellectual qualities | Beliefs and expectations | Expectations |
| 1. Intellectual qualities | Beliefs and expectations | Positive mindset |
| 1. Intellectual qualities | Beliefs and expectations | Positive perspective |

process. As the team encountered varied terminology representing similar concepts, relevant terms were incorporated into the codebook. Table 3.3 provides an example of the different key words that researchers may encounter during the coding process, and which indicator they could be coded against. This resource became pivotal for maintaining uniformity in the coding across team members engaged with the dataset.

## 3  Results

### 3.1  Selection of sources of evidence

The initial database search yielded 33,795 publications, which were downloaded to Endnote 20, then exported to Covidence for screening. Covidence automatically removed 12,941 duplicates, leaving 20,854

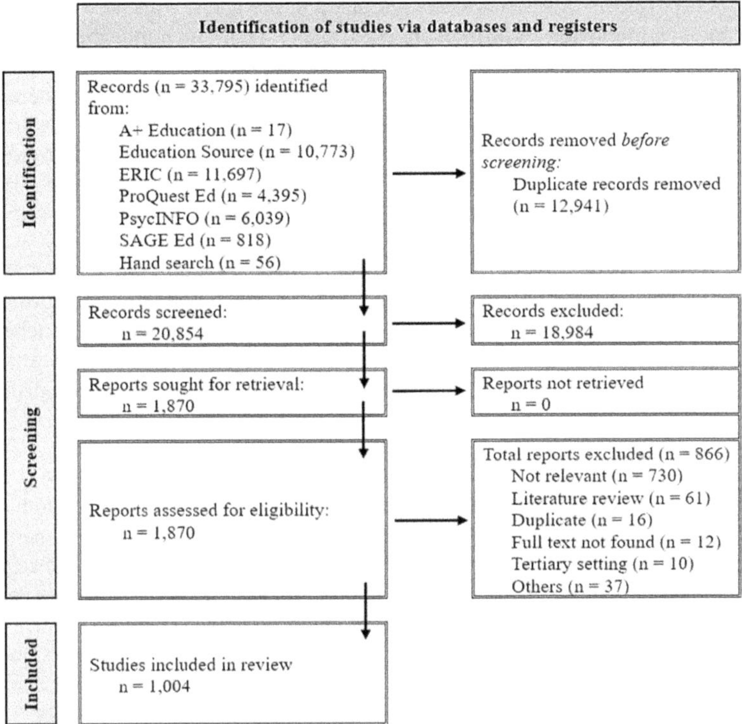



*Figure 3.1* Flow of information through the distinct phases of the scoping review

publications. The scoping review team manually screened these titles and abstracts, excluding 18,984 for reasons such as duplicates not initially identified, irrelevant populations (e.g., focusing on early childhood or tertiary educators), and inappropriate study designs (e.g., those not investigating teacher quality indicators).

Of the 1,870 publications subjected to full-text review, 866 were further excluded due to being opinion pieces, not in English, providing only summaries, or being editorials. Ultimately, 1,004 publications were identified as relevant and included for data extraction, focusing on the study's country, methods, population, and teacher quality indicators. The detailed screening and selection process is illustrated in Figure 3.1.

## 3.2 Characteristics of sources of evidence

The largest study included in this review involved 503,146 students from 69 countries, evaluating student measures of science teaching quality (Aditomo & Köhler, 2020). More than 32% of the included publications incorporated studies that were conducted in the USA, with the next most prevalent reported country being Australia (7.4%). The publications overwhelmingly focused on primary (31.7%), secondary (37.1%), or mixed (23.2%) contexts, with around 8% of study populations being undetermined (e.g. The participants were described as 'teachers' without specifying their schooling level context). The most common methodological approach involved qualitative designs, with 51% (N=509) of the studies utilising data collection approaches that included interviews, focus groups, and qualitative questionnaires.

The research cited in the publications collected data from a range of educational stakeholders, including teachers, school leaders, educational consultants, students, and parents. It also examined aspects of teacher quality related to all disciplines, including mathematics, science, creative arts, human society and its environment (HSIE), languages, and English.

### 3.3  *Critical appraisal within sources of evidence*

During the critical appraisal phase, validation data were extracted from a sample of 730 of the 1,004 included (72.7%). The process involved 11 members of the research team manually extracting validation evidence from the publications and entering them into a spreadsheet. The process was repeated for all 730 publications by a trained research assistant. There was a 97.1% level of agreement between the 11 researchers and the research assistant. This is considered almost perfect by Landis and Koch (1977). Where discrepancies did occur, consensus was reached through further discussion.

The critical appraisal of the publications revealed that in only 33% (N=241) of the publications, the author(s) stated evidence to support their measurement instruments validity and procedures. This highlights the need for authors to fully report their methods, including the validity and reliability of their instruments.

### 3.4  *Results of individual sources of evidence*

In total, 3,370 points of data related to indicators of teacher quality were extracted from 1,004 individual publications. Most publications reported on one indicator of teacher quality, while the largest contribution came from Jha (2011) which provided 110 points of extracted data. [see https://www.sydney.edu.au/arts/our-research/research-projects/teacher-quality/whats-the-evidence.html for further information]

### 3.5  *Synthesis of results*

To validate the coding process, all included publications authored by individuals with surnames from H to Z (constituting 63% of the total) were coded independently by two team members, achieving an agreement rate of 96%. Discrepancies were resolved through discussion, often involving consultation of the original publications to refine data point descriptions until consensus was achieved.

This final synthesis of results identified 3,370 discrete data points across the included publications. Each data point was then mapped to one of the four indicator components relating to the Teacher Quality Construct: Intellectual, Interpersonal, Affective, and Intrapersonal. This process successfully categorised 56.6% of the data points. However, the remaining 43.4% did not fit within these existing categories, leading to the introduction of three additional components:

- Pedagogical Qualities (Pedagogical skills and content knowledge essential for high-quality instruction [Park & Oliver, 2008; Shulman, 1987]),
- External Influences (encompassing classroom climate, school culture, and student-related factors), and
- Qualifications and Experience.

Table 3.4 shows the total number of extracted data points that were coded into each indicator of teacher quality.

Of the four components that comprise the Teacher Quality Construct, the strongest presence in the coded data came from the Interpersonal component (23.1%). These are indicators of teacher quality that are relevant to the ways in which teachers communicate with, interact with, and understand others, particularly their students. Of all the indicators in this component, collaboration and relationship building contained the greatest number of extracted data points (7.2%) across all four components. Publications coded to this indicator explored the importance of teacher-student relationships (White, 2020), teacher collaborative practice (Yuan et al., 2018), and the value of establishing connections with students and the broader community (Beykont, 2013). Other prevalent interpersonal indicators were communication, motivation/commitment, and self-efficacy.

Affective indicators were also highly prevalent in the coded data, comprising just over 17.8% of all extracted data. The strongest indicator was values and attitudes, which contained 4.4% of all extracted data. The research team defined this indicator as what teachers consider to be important and how they feel about professional issues (values), as well how they conduct themselves or are perceived to conduct themselves (attitudes). Just over a quarter of the extracted data in this indicator were related to a having a positive or optimistic attitude, including 'excitement about learning', 'passion and enthusiasm', and 'loving and respectful of students'. The literature coded into the values and attitudes indicator came from 38 countries, as well as two multi-country studies.

*Table 3.4* Teacher quality components, indicators, and total counts of extracted data from all included publications

| Indicator component | Indicators | Total |
| --- | --- | --- |
| **Intellectual qualities** | Analytical | 31 |
| | Beliefs and expectations | 39 |
| | Cognition | 33 |
| | Creativity | 57 |
| | Curiosity | 13 |
| | Decision making | 7 |
| | Judgement | 4 |
| | Logic and reasoning | 1 |
| | Problem solving | 14 |
| | Reflective practice | 56 |
| **Interpersonal qualities** | Adaptability | 52 |
| | Advocacy | 29 |
| | Agency | 25 |
| | Collaboration and relationship building | 246 |
| | Communication | 148 |
| | Influence | 51 |
| | Leadership | 44 |
| | Motivation/commitment | 110 |
| | Self-efficacy | 73 |
| **Affective qualities** | Collegiality | 64 |
| | Cultural competence | 65 |
| | Empathetic | 33 |
| | Morals and ethics | 19 |
| | Negotiation and conflict management | 16 |
| | Respect for difference and diversity | 119 |
| | Social and Emotional intelligence | 89 |
| | Social awareness | 45 |
| | Values and attitudes | 150 |
| **Intrapersonal qualities** | Initiative | 7 |
| | Patience | 12 |
| | Persistence | 12 |
| | Resilience | 26 |
| | Self-awareness | 29 |
| | Self-confidence | 33 |
| | Self-discipline | 142 |
| | Self-evaluation | 4 |
| | Time management | 10 |
| **External influences** | Environment | 124 |
| | Parents | 6 |
| | Research abilities | 9 |
| | Students | 42 |
| **Pedagogical qualities** | Knowledge: Assessment | 46 |
| | Knowledge: Behaviour management | 88 |
| | Knowledge: Content | 192 |
| | Knowledge: Context | 53 |
| | Knowledge: ICT | 74 |
| | Knowledge: Students | 8 |
| | Knowledge: Teaching practice | 594 |
| **Qualifications and experience** | Experience | 72 |
| | Qualifications | 154 |

The two components of intellectual and intrapersonal qualities were the least prevalent (7.6% and 8.2% respectively) in the coded data, with both components combined making up just over a quarter of all extracted data. Within these components, the indicator of self-discipline contained the most coded data (4.2%) highlighting the importance of characteristics like professionalism, diligence, and accountability, and included studies from 38 different countries.

Another point of interest regarding the publications identified for this scoping review was the increasing prevalence and interest in indicators of teacher quality across the 10-year span. The number of identified publications grew from 50 identified in 2011, through to 115 identified in 2020, with the number peaking at 123 in 2018. This shows that educational researchers around the globe have a growing interest and focus on teacher quality, and are increasingly exploring the nature of teacher quality beyond 'value-add' measures or student outcomes. However, the number of publications dropped back to 58 in 2021. While it is not possible to determine why this is the case, it is possible to see that much of the research conducted in this area involves interaction with teachers, students, and schools – something which became very difficult to do in 2020 during the Covid-19 pandemic. This may have made it hard for researchers to effectively investigate teacher quality, drawing their interests and efforts elsewhere.

Among the three additional components that emerged during the analysis, (i.e., pedagogical qualities, external influences, and qualifications and experience), pedagogical qualities were the most prevalent, accounting for 31.3%, with teaching practice being the most frequently extracted indicator within that category.

While listing the prevalence of the indicators is important, it is critical to note that the number of times an indicator appears in our scoping review is not equivalent to its relative significance to the construct of teacher quality, as indicators may reflect common research themes or accessible data rather than an indicator's fundamental importance or impact on teacher quality. Just as notable as what was highly prevalent in the data were the indicators that received the least number of extracted data. Indicators with 10 or fewer extracted data points included time management, initiative, and self-evaluation (intrapersonal qualities), and decision making, judgement, and logic and reasoning (intellectual qualities). It is not possible determine why certain indicators are more or less prevalent than others, only that the parameters of the scoping review yielded these results. Future research explicitly focused on these indicators may return a more comprehensive field of publications.

## 4 Discussion

### *4.1 Summary of evidence*

Our deliberate focus in this chapter has been to seek current and detailed evidence of how teacher quality is represented in educational research and to provide a clear evidence base on which the profession can argue its case for greater recognition. To our knowledge, this is the first review to provide a comprehensive overview of indicators of teacher quality from numerous theoretical perspectives. The range of extracted data points from this scoping review indicate that teacher quality is complex and varied, and supports a multitude of qualities that are valued in different educational contexts. Though researchers have previously found it difficult to identify characteristics that predict teacher quality (Biesta et al., 2015; Darling-Hammond, 2000; Gilmore & Kramer, 2019; Haddix, 2015), our findings demonstrate a predominant proportion of teacher (60%) versus teaching (40%) qualities identified in the literature. The scoping review has established an evidence base for potential investigations into important issues such as how judgements of teacher quality are made through measures of teaching quality. The dual themes of measurement and support are discussed briefly below in terms of practical outcomes and future considerations.

### *4.1.1 Practical outcomes*

This scoping review indicates that there are many facets to teacher quality as well as many measures used to assess it. The practical outcomes from this work encourage educational stakeholders to explore the nature of teacher quality from all stages of teacher development.

Currently, initial teacher education (ITE) providers wishing to attract high-quality candidates into teaching adopt a variety of processes to assess candidates' suitability to teach. The concept of "readiness for the profession" (Sachs, 2000) acknowledges the breadth of practice in a teacher's role and relates to the full range of teacher quality attributes. The term 'classroom ready' was first introduced by Darling-Hammond, Wise and Klein in 1995 when they claimed that performance assessments "provide the possibility of more successfully judging prospective teachers' readiness to teach" (Darling-Hammond et al., 1995, p. 4). Australian ITE accreditation policies mandate the requirement of establishing the 'classroom readiness' of preservice teachers at graduation, determined by the successful completion of a TPA and supported by strong degree program validity evidence (Stacey et al., 2019). To ensure there can be growth across an ITE program in order to produce effective, high-quality graduate teachers, we suggest that the indicators of teacher quality that form our Teacher Quality Construct could be used to inform a profile assessment at point of entry into a degree program, as well as support the development of teaching performance assessments (TPAs) that measure a graduate's readiness to move into the classroom. As no evidence base exists yet to measure the predictive validity of TPAs as a 'fit for purpose' measurement of classroom readiness, the Teacher Quality Construct could be adopted for that purpose.

Teacher professional development programs could also be aligned with the Teacher Quality Construct to promote a holistic scaffold for capacity building as teachers in the field seek to improve their professional quality. This developmental approach to teacher education views the work involved in becoming a teacher as part of a continuum of connected learning that commences in ITE programs and continues through teachers' professional engagement in the classroom and in-service professional learning (Darling-Hammond, 2012; Day, 2017).

By identifying a research base for indicators of teacher quality, this study supports teacher educators worldwide in enhancing the validity of teacher assessment models at a time when the quality of teachers is frequently questioned. It also initiates a process to gather evidence that can contribute to the ongoing debate regarding the quality of teachers in education systems globally. Furthermore, this study underscores the necessity of developing robust measures for these indicators to ensure their effectiveness and reliability in assessing teacher quality.

## 4.2 *Limitations*

This scoping review has several limitations. To make the review feasible for the research team, only publications written in English were included in the review, and only publications in the stated date range were included. Whilst possible researcher bias may have had an influence during the coding process, particularly around the different understandings and interpretations of the original outcome variables reported in included publications, this was minimised with double appraisal and inter-rater reliability.

Although the components and indicators of our Teacher Quality Construct make it possible to describe research-informed profiles of teacher quality, we note: (1) there will not be one 'best' version of a teacher, but rather there will potentially be subtly nuanced combinations of indicators which account for personal and contextual differences; and (2) there will be change over time. This scoping review presents a perspective on teacher quality informed by research published during the years 2011–2021. This perspective may change as teachers, teaching, and educational research continues to evolve.

## 5 Conclusion

The review has provided insight into the complex process of identifying existing indicators of teacher quality and demonstrated how evidence of those indicators can be collected in a rigorous manner. It is supporting the creation of an evidence-based Teacher Quality Construct, which includes the four components examined in detail in this paper: intellectual qualities, interpersonal qualities, affective qualities, and intrapersonal qualities. Developing a research-informed understanding of these indicators may benefit education systems by providing clear guidelines for quality, potentially enhancing teacher job satisfaction and retention. Therefore, this scoping review lays the foundation for further research.

However, the review highlights that the evidence primarily reflects what is easier to measure, not necessarily what is important. For instance, while interpersonal qualities were most prevalent, intellectual qualities like decision making and reasoning, which are central to teaching, were less represented. This suggests a need for future studies to explore ways to measure all aspects of teacher quality comprehensively.

In addition, the study demonstrates how scoping reviews can significantly impact the initial stages of defining a construct by providing a comprehensive overview of the existing literature and identifying the key components that should be included. This logical approach allows for a more informed and nuanced understanding of complex constructs. Furthermore, scoping reviews facilitate the refinement of these constructs by highlighting gaps in current research and suggesting areas where further investigation or more precise definitions are needed (Davis et al., 2009). This iterative process of concept building and refinement enhances the clarity and applicability of a construct in subsequent research and practice.

The results have implications for professional practice and policy, particularly in supporting early career teachers and informing ITE programs. However, to effect systemic change, fit for purpose, and validated measures of all relevant qualities must be developed. These measurable indicators could be applied to check the predictive validity of TPAs and guide professional development, although it is essential to recognise that TPAs offer only partial insights into a teacher candidate's potential.

The findings reframe what constitutes teacher quality, which may lead to better teaching practices and improved student outcomes, aligning with global efforts to support teachers and the teaching profession (United Nations Educational Scientific and Cultural Organization, 2022).

## Key References


Clinton, J. M., Koelle, M., & Aston, R. (2018). *Investigating the key determinants of effective teaching: A systematic review.* The University of Melbourne.

Grönqvist, E., & Vlachos, J. (2016). One size fits all? The effects of teachers' cognitive and social abilities on student achievement. *Labour Economics, 42*, 138–150. https://doi.org/10.1016/j.labeco.2016.08.005

Hopkins, D., & Stern, D. (1996). Quality teachers, quality schools: International perspectives and policy implications. *Teaching and Teacher Education, 12* (5), 501–517. https://doi.org/10.1016/0742-051X (95)00055-O

Peters, M. D. J., Marnie, C., Tricco, A. C., Pollock, D., Munn, Z., Alexander, L., McInerney, P., Godfrey, C. M., & Khalil, H. (2020). Updated methodological guidance for the conduct of scoping reviews. *JBI Evidence Synthesis, 18* (10), 2119–2126. https://doi.org/10.11124/ JBIES-20-00167

Simpson, A., Cotton, W., & Gore, J. (2021). Teacher education/ors in Australia: Still shaping the profession despite policy intervention. In D. Mayer (Ed.), *Teacher education policy and research: Global perspectives* (pp. 11–25). Springer. https://doi.org/10.1007/978-981-16-3775-9_2

Tricco, A. C., Lillie, E., Zarin, W., O'Brien, K. K., Colquhorn, H., Levac, D., Moher, D., Peters, M. D. J., Horsley, T., Weeks, L., Hempel, S., Akl, E. A., Chang, C., McGowan, J., Stewart, L., Hartling, L., Aldcroft, A., Wilson, M. G., Garritty, C., Straus, S. E. (2018). PRISMA extension for scoping reviews (PRISMA-ScR): Checklist and explanation. *Annals of Internal Medicine, 169*(7), 467–473. https://doi.org/10.7326/M18-0850

# 4 Confirming the Teacher Quality Construct using a modified Delphi process

*Alyson Simpson, Damian Maher, George Harb, and Anne Lawson-Jones*

## Introduction

The What's the Evidence (WtE) study is a deliberate attempt to nuance the narrative about teacher quality, representing it as a recognised construct that is valued and supported by the profession and informed by scholarly research. The research highlights the difficulty of defining and measuring teacher quality and fills a gap in the field, creating an evidence base for a shared framework for identifying and supporting indicators of teacher quality. In this chapter we discuss how expert stakeholders responded to discussion of the indicators belonging to the four components helping to confirm the construct as fit-for-purpose for the profession.

This chapter presents the rationale and outcomes of adopting a modified Delphi process of data collection from a panel of expert stakeholders. We report on the process used to provide evidence to support the research and stakeholder informed Teacher Quality Construct that is influenced by a general theory of self that borrows from sociological and psychological models of identity (Davis et al., 2019; Stets & Burke, 2000). The development of teacher quality is a progressive, cumulative, and complex process that commences during initial teacher education and continues throughout a teacher's career (Day, 2017). Our study focusses specifically on early career teachers (ECTs) as a group of teachers as that career phase is associated worldwide with high attrition rates (Amitai & Van Houtte, 2022). In Australia, the ECT phase commences with assessment against professional standards using teaching performance assessment (TPA) measurement instruments.

Research question (RQ) 1 of the WtE study asks: What indicators of teacher quality are identified by stakeholders and the literature as relevant to early career teachers? The scoping review reported in Chapter 3 answered the second part of the RQ through an examination of recent, relevant literature. This chapter addresses the first part of the RQ by discussing the complex nature of teacher quality with Australian educational

DOI: 10.4324/9781003542575-4

stakeholders. Through our analysis of their discussion, we reveal how stakeholders respond to the construct of teacher quality we propose.

As noted in Chapter 1, the Teacher Quality Construct created for this study refers to a composite of characteristics and attributes, knowledges and intelligences possessed, developed and practised reflexively by an individual. The construct represents teacher qualities as:

**Intellectual**: A teacher's cognitive processing abilities, which equates to a professional mind-set;
**Interpersonal**: The ways in which teachers communicate with, interact with, and understand others, including community members but particularly their students;
**Affective**: The teacher's capacity to be relatable e.g., empathetic; and
**Intrapersonal**: A teacher's ability to take personal responsibility for professional conduct.

Previous studies have examined varied indicators singly or in groups but never from the holistic, integrative approach that we have taken. Please refer to Chapter 3 for the evidence base for our Teacher Quality Construct that synthesised an extensive body of literature.

In the modified Delphi process we asked stakeholders to consider which of the 37 indicators included in the four components that made up the Teacher Quality Construct they deemed to be most essential for ECTs (i.e., 1–5 years post-graduation). By examining the expectations stakeholders place on ECTs through the lens of identity theory, our findings demonstrate the critical importance of a growth mindset for teacher professional development. We note that some qualities that stakeholders value may be "difficult to define and measure" (Scott et al., 2012, p. 4). However, work that expands understanding of the overall construct of teacher quality will provide a valuable contribution to efforts to measure the multi-dimensional complexity of teacher quality (McColskey et al., 2006).

Our approach to the challenge of defining teacher quality takes into account the complexity inherent in discussing how ECTs are assessed in their first few years post-graduation by those who have long standing experience in the profession. Because identity theory proposes that individuals change and adapt to cultural and social pressures as they play out their roles in different contexts across time, we have adopted it as a theoretical frame for our study. Identity theory acknowledges that teacher identity is dynamic, dialogical, and affected by context (Hanna et al., 2019). Framing our study in identity theory allows us to attend not only to the individual/personal, but also to the groups to which they belong (e.g. ECTs), and the roles they undertake (e.g. as teacher) which will be impacted by the contexts in which they teach (Burke & Stets, 2023; Stets & Serpe, 2013). This theoretical framework suits our methodology as we analyse how stakeholder perceptions of ECTs are based on "shared expectations attached to social positions in society" (Stets & Serpe, 2013, p. 38). In understanding teacher quality and considering teacher professional learning, it is important to understand that teachers' identities, and their qualities, are supported through engagement with other teachers, students, parents, and the broader community.

## Methodology: Delphi process

As outlined in Chapter 2, the Delphi process is best known as "an unbiased process to solicit opinions and reach consensus in an area where there is no clear evidence for the solution to the problem under consideration" (Santaguida et al., 2018, p. 9), making it suitable for the exploratory nature of the WtE study. The most common design features of the methodology include anonymous data collection, iterative rounds of data collection, and synthesis of feedback between rounds (two to three rounds is the norm) with the goal of achieving consensus as survey items are reduced during the process (Rowe & Wright, 2011). Positive design features of the Delphi process include avoidance of peer pressure on decision making as all participants receive summarised opinions. The process allows for all views to be collected without biased intervention from the researchers.

The key purpose for using the Delphi method is to enable the collection of a range of "informed judgments on issues that are largely unexplored, difficult to define, highly context and expertise specific, or future-oriented" (Fletcher & Marchildon, 2014, p. 3). Given the disparate views that exist on the contested concept of what counts as 'quality' in teacher quality and the need to create a list of indicators that is relevant to the local context, a Delphi methodology was chosen as suitable for the phase of the WtE study following the scoping review. However, we wanted to confirm the professional relevance of our construct of teacher quality with leaders in the profession before we ran survey cycles with the broader participant population. So, we adopted a modified Delphi process and introduced a step of consultation with an expert panel. This approach is supported by research where expert determined weighting of indicators has led to more refined construct development that is relevant to the stakeholders (Lu, 2012).

The modified Delphi process employed for this study specifically includes direct consultation with key stakeholders on survey items as an initial step prior to the broader study population completing any surveys (von der Gracht, 2012). We designed into our study a step where an expert panel of stakeholder participants completed a survey and then met in small focus groups to consider the inherent logic of the construct by examining the synthesised results. Data collected from the expert panel, which include focus group commentary on their combined survey results, were analysed for the relevance experts perceived of the teacher quality indicators in relation to ECTs. Through the findings we appraised experts' confirmation of our construct of teacher quality to challenge and/or stabilise it.

## Participants

Sixteen expert panel participants for Phase 2 were recruited from colleagues who have knowledge of the NSW education system including the Australian Professional Standards for Teachers (APST) and have teaching, policy or research experience in the NSW Department of Education or professionally affiliated bodies. These characteristics ensured representation from a broad range of different perspectives. Our expert panel of stakeholders included employers, accrediting bodies, the Australian Federal Government education agency related to teachers and teacher quality, and other key industry leaders. During our discussion of the findings the identity of the participants has been anonymised. Each participant was given a code representing the focus group they attended and a name reference. For example, [FG1A] represents participant A who attended focus group 1.

### *Data collection*

Two tools were used to collect data from the Delphi expert panel stakeholder group. The first was an online survey, which was developed from the information extracted from the scoping review and included all the indicators of teacher quality within the four components. Table 4.1 displays the terms that were included in the survey listed in alphabetical order. The Qualtrics interactive survey design included a drop-down definition for each indicator derived from the scoping review work that could be accessed within the survey to assist with shared understanding. In the survey panel members were asked to rank the indicators in each category according to their perceived relative importance for ECTs. Options for ranking included essential, very desirable, somewhat desirable, and not relevant. The survey also allowed participants to add extra indicators where they believed it was necessary at the end of each component list in an open field.

### *Survey results*

The survey results for each participant were analysed for percentage weighting by indicator as judged by relevance to ECTs. The overall scores were then synthesised into rankings showing group prioritisation of

*Table 4.1* Indicators in the four components

| Intellectual | Interpersonal | Affective | Intrapersonal |
| --- | --- | --- | --- |
| Analytical | Adaptability | Collegiality | Initiative |
| Beliefs and | Advocacy | Cultural | Patience |
| expectations | Agency | competence | Persistence |
| Cognition | Collaboration and | Empathetic | Resilience |
| Creativity | relationship | Morals and ethics | Self-awareness |
| Curiosity | building | Negotiation | Self-confidence |
| Decision making | Communication | and conflict | Self-discipline |
| Judgement | Influence | management | Self-evaluation |
| Logic and | Leadership | Respect for | Time management |
| reasoning | Motivation/ | difference and | |
| Problem solving | commitment | diversity | |
| Reflective | Self-efficacy | Social and | |
| practice | | Emotional | |
| | | intelligence | |
| | | Social awareness | |
| | | Values and | |
| | | attitudes | |

indicator relevance. Table 4.2 provides a summary of how the indicators were ranked by the expert panel according to the survey results. NB: No items were recorded as not relevant so there are no items recorded in that column.

### Focus groups

The second data collection tool adopted was online focus group discussion of the professional 'fit' of the construct components. As no common time could be found to suit all participants, two focus groups were held on two different occasions on Zoom. Each participant attended only one of the focus group discussions, which took approximately 60 minutes. Both focus groups followed the same process of allowing time for issues to be raised by the participants relating to their perceived relevance to ECTs of the indicators in each of the components. As conversations were recorded with informed consent, the researchers were able to report on spoken commentary from the focus groups.

As each of the stakeholder participants had completed the online survey prior to attending a focus group, they were all familiar with the components and had made their own individual judgements of indicator ranking as relevant to ECTs. Padlet, an online interactive noticeboard, was employed in the focus groups to display the collated results from the survey of the entire panel. The Padlet screen displayed the results for each component arranged in columns ranked as essential, very desirable, somewhat desirable, and not relevant. Each indicator was represented on screen as a

*Table 4.2* Results of stakeholder survey collating results from all the panel members

| Component | Essential | Very desirable | Somewhat desirable | Not relevant |
|---|---|---|---|---|
| **Intellectual** | Cognition | Analytical Curiosity Creativity Problem solving Reflective practice | Judgement Logic and reasoning Beliefs and expectations Decision making | |
| **Interpersonal** | Adaptability Communication | Agency Advocacy Self-efficacy Leadership Influence | Motivation and commitment Collaboration and relationship building | |
| **Affective** | Respect for difference and diversity Morals and ethics | Negotiation and conflict management Collegiality Empathy Cultural competence | Social emotional intelligence Social awareness Values and attitudes | |
| **Intrapersonal** | Resilience Persistence | Initiative Self-discipline Self-awareness | Self-confidence Self-evaluation Patience Time management | |

coloured tile of blue, green or yellow. The colours signalled the prioritisation results after the survey where blue = Essential, green = Very Desirable, yellow = Somewhat Desirable. The visual information served as a provocation for discussion to help participants build shared understanding as they worked towards confirmation of the construct. If the panel members' comments indicated that rankings should change because of discussions, the focus group host moved the indicators around on screen. At the end of the meeting the Padlet screen revealed indicators that had moved higher or lower in the rankings. The research team informed the panel that the indicator names were extracted from the literature noting that identification of problematic terms could lead to changed survey items in future follow up studies. Justifications given by the panel members for changes or additions to the indicators were audio recorded. The key points arising from these discussions are reported below in the findings under component headings. Through these discussions we also gained valuable insight to experts' perceptions of what contributes to the formation of ECTs identity as teachers.

## Focus group results

The focus group data have been thematically analysed below under the headings of the four components: intellectual, interpersonal, affective, and intrapersonal qualities. The researchers note in particular where definitional contention arose and how it was resolved during discussion as that demonstrated the process of consensus at work. It gives insight to the debates that emerged as experts simultaneously considered

a. which indicators they believed need to be prioritised as essential when supporting the development of ECTs and
b. the appropriateness of the construct as a representation of teacher quality.

As a result of their discussions the expert panel stakeholder consultation identified twelve potential indicators of teacher quality as being essential for ECTs. These are:

* cognition, curiosity, and belief and expectations (intellectual component)
* adaptability, communication, and collaboration and relationship building (interpersonal component)
* respect for difference and diversity, morals and ethics, and cultural competence (affective component)
* resilience, persistence, and time management (intrapersonal component)

At the top of each subsection a table is included showing the resulting shift in prioritisation of indicators relevant to early career teachers as judged by the expert panel across the component being discussed. The colours from the original Padlets are represented by font style where Essential = **bold**, Very Desirable = <u>underlined</u>, Somewhat Desirable = *italics* and plain font = indicator did not change from less than essential. The tables reveal that all indicators originally listed as Essential in the survey results remained classified as Essential. However, three indicators originally listed as Very Desirable in the survey results were reprioritised as Essential and two indicators originally listed as Somewhat Desirable in the survey results were reprioritised as Essential. In our reporting below we discuss only those indicators that prompted extensive commentary from panel members.

### *Intellectual qualities*

The focus groups agreed that the component of intellectual quality should encourage understanding of the constant complexity of the classroom that requires teachers to problem-solve consistently and to make micro-decisions regularly on a daily basis, which depend on professional judgements (Table 4.3). Across both focus groups there was unified agreement that Cognition should be signalled as essential as the indicator was seen as fundamental to the enactment of all other qualities in the category needed to build future teaching capacity. Comments such as: "You've got to have some intellectual capability at the start as the basis for building the rest of those things on" [FG1L] and "If you don't have that intellectual base, you're not going to learn that along the way, and that base enables you to build your teaching capacity" [FG1J] clearly align with the research that suggests a teacher's intellectual capacity is key to student learning (Bardach & Klassen, 2020; Stronge, 2007).

Within this component indicators that shifted included Curiosity and Beliefs and expectations. The discussion around the importance of Curiosity, which moved from very desirable to essential, was underpinned by comments such as "I do look for bucket loads of curiosity in an early career teacher. I want them to know that they're going to learn and grow by observing others" [FG1M]. This view was supported by others who saw Curiosity as an underpinning necessity for ECTs. "If you're not out there hungry to know stuff, then you're not going to build that creativity. You've got to have that curiosity sitting there" [FG1L]. The same opinion was voiced in focus group 2 where Curiosity was read as a synonym for reflective practice, which was seen as "a hundred percent essential for teachers" [FG2Tf]. In short, consensus was reached by the stakeholders, but they recognise that the possibility for ECTs to maintain Curiosity is challenging.

It was clear in panel members' discussions that some terms needed to be clarified to avoid confusion. For example, comments on why Beliefs and expectations should move from somewhat desirable to essential demonstrated two different interpretations existed. Some experts interpreted the indicator to refer to the belief teachers had of their student potential. This discussion aligns with the literature on the impact of self-fulfilling predictions that avows the connection between teachers'

*Table 4.3* Indicator movement after focus group discussion of the intellectual component

| *Final state: essential* | *Final state: very desirable* | *Final state: somewhat desirable* | *Final state: not relevant* |
|---|---|---|---|
| **Cognition** | Analytical | Judgement | |
| *Curiosity* | Creativity | Logic and reasoning | |
| *Beliefs and expectations* | Problem solving | Decision making | |
| | Reflective practice | | |

beliefs about students and student learning outcomes. This group argued for positioning belief in student potential as an essential part of a teacher's "DNA" [FG1M]. It needs to inform the teacher's work so that "every child can learn, be engaged, prosper, can be nurtured" [FG1M] no matter what level of disadvantage they may face. This perspective contrasted with the way other panel members read the term as referring to a teacher's personal beliefs, e.g., political or religious. Their ranking of the indicator originally had been low as they did not believe a teacher should deliberately "transfer political, cultural, religious, social beliefs which are very subjective onto students" [FG1C]. Once [FG1C] realised the intended meaning of the indicator they fully agreed with its essential nature for ECTs and its relevance to the construct.

### Interpersonal qualities

As with the Intellectual component, in the Interpersonal component there were some indicators that the panel accepted without question, and they remained in the essential column (Table 4.4). For example, Communication was named as core to how early career teachers demonstrate their ability to relate to students, colleagues and community members. One of the experts stated

> I just would have to say there's no way in the world that communication can't be there. It's just so fundamental that a teacher is able to communicate in a range of ways with their students and with their colleagues.
>
> [FG1L]

This comment drew strong affirmation from the group and no further discussion of the term ensued. Knoell et al.'s research exploring how positive student – teacher social relationships are built supports the

*Table 4.4* Indicator movement after focus group discussion of the interpersonal component

| *Final state: essential* | *Final state: very desirable* | *Final state: somewhat desirable* | *Final state: not relevant* |
| --- | --- | --- | --- |
| **Adaptability** | Agency | Motivation and | |
| **Communication** | Advocacy | commitment | |
| *Collaboration and relationship building* | Self-efficacy | | |
| | Leadership | | |
| | Influence | | |

experts' consensus view as it notes the importance of active listening as a key communicative tool that influences learning (2015).

Within this component, greater emphasis was raised in the discussion on the importance of Collaboration and relationship building over other indicators. All participants agreed that these two items were so valuable as qualities that they should move two columns from somewhat desirable into the essential column. This shift was influenced by stakeholders who commented on both the critical nature and also the challenges that ECTs have in developing these qualities. Our panel members viewed Collaboration as critical for the ECT to develop the ability to grow, noting how "Working with other early career teachers in a collaborative way can be really effective" [FG1L]. They also recommended that ECTs should not act as 'sole traders' because they need to relate to a range of individuals and collaborate with others to learn. However, it was noted that relationship building can be difficult for beginning teachers especially at the start when they are working out the existing power dynamics in a school, for example, in the staffroom or when working with more experienced teachers.

Challenges were identified where early career teachers are expected to build relationships and be collaborative with more experienced teachers, yet these potential mentors "are not necessarily that open and willing to do that" [FG1L]. Newberry (2010) suggests that initial teacher education programs include some preparation to mitigate the risk of ECTs not developing professional interpersonal relationships. This work would address the concerns the panel raised that it takes time to develop relationships and that this would not occur unless collaboration is supported from the ground up. The focus of discussion was largely on collaboration with other teachers; however, attention was also paid to students. "You're in an industry where you're daily intersecting with adults and the kids. You've got to be able to collaborate and share and learn, and you got to build relationships with staff and students" [FG1M]. The literature on Collaboration and relationship building emphasises the need for teachers to pay attention to the human element of teaching (Alzobiani, 2020), given the interweaving of relationships with all members of school communities including staff, students and parents and carers (Straková et al., 2018).

### *Affective qualities*

Though the indicators were all highly valued, this component caused the most conflict around use of terminology (Table 4.5). While the panel agreed that the term Cultural competence should be moved from very desirable to essential, in-depth discussion revealed discomfort with use of the term. An Aboriginal participant noted that "cultural competence is a term that is a little bit tricky at the moment" and suggested another term should be considered such as "cultural responsiveness, cultural humility,

*Table 4.5* Indicator movement after focus group discussion of the affective component

| Final state: essential | Final state: very desirable | Final state: somewhat desirable | Final state: not relevant |
|---|---|---|---|
| **Respect for difference and diversity** **Morals and ethics** *Cultural competence* | Negotiation and conflict management Collegiality Empathy | Social emotional intelligence Social awareness Values and attitudes | |

cultural, etc., etc." [FG2C]. The use of the term 'cultural competence' is continually debated in the literature (Chavez, 2012), as by definition a person could be judged culturally incompetent, and perhaps not equipped to interact professionally with members of particular groups. In its place 'cultural responsiveness' has emerged as a term within an Australian context informed by a founding commitment to expand teachers' pedagogical opportunities in relationship with all students, but particularly with Aboriginal and Torres Strait Islander students (Australian Institute for Teaching and School Leadership, 2022; Morrison et al., 2019). To recalibrate the quality as more appropriate to current understandings the expert panel suggested that the term Cultural competence be amended to *Cultural responsiveness* or *Cultural humility*.

Within this component there was also lively debate around the use of the term Respect for difference and diversity. The challenge of defining this term was highlighted by one participant: "It's always a difficult one to define... a difficult quality to capture in words" [FG2CS]. The use of the term 'difference' was seen as problematic. One member noted "there may be a very good reason why you're using the word difference but, from my perspective, wouldn't we just be respecting diversity rather than highlighting difference? To me, it's a bit pejorative" [FG2A]. One of the suggestions to reduce confusion was to rename the indicator Respect for diversity. The experts' comments echo research that reveals challenges with sense making about difference and diversity impacts on inclusive and equitable practices in schools (Pollock & Briscoe, 2019).

The third term to stimulate debate was Morals and ethics, which was agreed to be essential to teacher quality, however, the combination of two terms in the one indicator was seen as problematic. One person felt that both the terms were important as indicated by this comment: "I agree they're both essential but I'm just not sure if that's expressed in a way that would not be contestable, I guess, is the best way I can to describe that" [FG2A]. The use of the word 'morals' was found to be problematic as suggested by the panel member: "I think we around this meeting would all agree it's quite subjective, isn't it?" [FG2A]. This was a highly respectful but challenging discussion because the misunderstandings and misconceptions around the concept of morals can hinder arrival at a 'correct' explanation (Chowdhury, 2018). After discussion the group felt that 'ethics' would be a more appropriate term to consider as a quality than morals and would be less open to judgemental appraisals. This change is being considered for later studies.

### *Intrapersonal qualities*

In this component the indicators were all seen to be relevant as "Early career teachers tell us the greatest support they get is from their peers so intrapersonal relationships are really important" [FG2A]. However, the panel discussion emphasised one indicator that was perceived as essential but contentiously named (Table 4.6). Resilience was named as problematic as noted by one member: "we really find the word resilience difficult; I'm going to be honest. Teachers are always told, just be resilient." [FG2A]. Given the problematic use of this term a member suggested: "I'm just putting in a flag for moving away from the word resilience" [FG2A]. The experts might have been more convinced of the appropriateness of the term if the conversation had been informed by research that supports a contextualised, social theory of resilience (Johnson et al., 2014). This body of work suggests that resilience should not be understood as purely a responsibility that ECTs should adopt. Rather, when viewed as "a process located at the interface of personal and contextual challenges and resources" (Mansfield et al., 2014, p. 547) issues such as reluctance to seek help, low levels of self-efficacy, concerns about content knowledge, and behaviour management would be managed with the support of school leadership.

Within this component emphasis was also placed on the essential nature of Time management as pressure on ECTs to manage time well can influence their decision to stay in the profession (Manuel & Carter, 2016). One member noted: "I can't see that time management isn't at least very

*Table 4.6* Indicator movement after focus group discussion of the intrapersonal component

| *Final state: essential* | *Final state: very desirable* | *Final state: somewhat desirable* | *Final state: not relevant* |
|---|---|---|---|
| **Resilience** | Initiative | Self-confidence | |
| **Persistence** | Self-discipline | Self-evaluation | |
| *Time management* | Self-awareness | | |
| | Patience | | |

desirable to survive and to be effective for yourself and your students" [FG2T]. As a result of discussion this item moved from very desirable into the essential column. The indicator of Patience was blended into the consideration of Time management as:

> A lot of the conflict in school, let's be honest about that, is when people are under pressure, time pressure and curriculum pressure and all the things on top of teachers, actually, patience in terms of interacting with their colleagues are actually essential.
>
> [FG2A]

A third indicator that drew out critical commentary from the panel in relation to ECTs was Self-evaluation. Researchers and teacher educators have argued that it is important to foster self-evaluation in order to produce qualified teachers (Liu, 2015). This point was discussed by the group as key to learning and, as opinions were canvassed, both positive and negative comments about how ECTs engage in Self-reflection emerged, so it remained in the somewhat desirable column. One participant commented: "You want them to have a reflective mindset, you want them to be reflecting on their experiences and practice" [FG1M]. Other participants noted, "We also want them to understand that they have a lot to learn from their peers, from their supervisors, from their principals… and not think you know everything right now, because you [have just] come out of uni" [FG2C]; and "if they're not engaging in the feedback that they receive and getting a sense of what to do with that, then that's going to be a problem" [FG1L].

## Discussion

Having presented the commentary from the focus groups in relation to indicator relevance, we now turn to examine the discussion through the lens of identity theory. We adopt the view of identity theory in that it addresses "the ways individuals perform and manage themselves as unique persons, role occupants, and group/social category members" (Davis et al., 2019, p. 256). This theoretical approach has helped us highlight the ways in which deliberations over teacher quality provided stakeholders with the opportunity to conceptualise the group of ECTs in relation to the role of teacher. We will discuss the concerns the panel members raised about the indicators in relation to the representation of ECTs that resulted from their language choices. We use the three identity types of self, role, and group/social (Burke & Stets, 2023) as thematic organisers. All three codes are relevant to discussions of ECT identity in the ecology of interactions between people, material conditions and system requirements though we note that there are far more identifiable instances of group and role identity formation being discussed than self.

## Self

There was one significant occasion when a personalised stance was adopted by an individual to critique an indicator term. When this occurred, the individual was arguing an ideological point from a position of their unique self. That is, the speaker was reflecting on their own lived experience informed by a specific cultural knowledge base expressing an opinion that was intensely meaningful to them. This contribution was important to the debate as it was aimed at correcting inappropriate terminology. It was one of the rare times when a panel member was not acting as a spokesperson for the group ECT or role of teacher. It is interesting to note that even though the expert panel members had previously been teachers at some point in their career, in this context they were considering the issue of teacher quality from a broader, systemic perspective rather than on the basis of their personal experience. That is, the self-identity type, which would have been prominent as an expression of an individual's evaluation of an experience (Akkerman & Meijer, 2011), was less visible in this discussion as the panel members were positioned as experts.

## Role

Stakeholders use the term 'teachers' to refer to the generic role of a person who is at no specific career stage but is therefore assumed to be not an ECT. Language such as "expect", "fundamental", "conflict" all used in direct commentary about teachers supports the view that teachers are recognised as occupying a social position in society that comes with professional expectations (Stets & Serpe, 2013). They are reported to have well developed "leadership" capacities, they are "accomplished", "resilient" and have "a range" of ways of adapting to student needs. There are also recognised challenges for teachers who may work in schools under "high pressure", but the overarching portrayal of idealised teacher identity is summed up in the statement "You've got to be able to collaborate and share and learn, and you got to build relationships with staff and students" [FG1M]. The stakeholders recognise the importance of teachers being "mentors" for ECTs as they progress through their careers to being considered as fully accomplished teachers. This highlights the responsibility loading that teachers carry when meeting the expectations of others in the multilayered political contexts and education systems in which they operate (Buchanan, 2015; Day, 2017).

In our study we refer to ECTs as a group as if they are a subset of the more generic role of teacher. We acknowledge that the separation of group from role we created for the purposes of discussion above is academic as we recognise that identity is "social, discontinuous, dialogical and multiple in nature" (Day, 2017, p. 50). However, the discussion has allowed us to examine the expectations stakeholders have of teacher quality in relation to ECTs, which contributes to our goal of building shared understandings.

### *Group*

The stakeholders explicitly used the classification of ECT as a linguistic tag to make it clear when they were referring to a particular group of professionals who are located at a time point at the start of their careers. Language such as "grow", "learn", "build", "develop", and "kicking off" all used in direct commentary about ECTs as a group supports the view of identity development as dynamic (Hanna et al., 2019). However, the discussion was not all positive with words such as "trouble", "risk of over cooking", "overwhelmed" and "how much is required" revealing stakeholder concern for the impact of contextual pressures on ECTs to survive. Fortunately, during their discussion stakeholders referred to qualities that could mitigate against these problems, using terms from the Teacher Quality Construct such as "curiosity", "collaboration", "reflective practice" and "creativity", which demonstrates the experts perceived their suitability for the context. The overarching portrayal of the ECT as summed up in the statement "some of those things you would want to mindfully delay" is evidence that experts understand that qualities can develop over time. We suggest there is clear evidence that the stakeholders understand the complexity of the profession that ECTs have entered and recognise that, as there is so much for an ECT to engage with, they should be well scaffolded and given time to allow teacher qualities to develop.

## Conclusion

In summary, the analysis of the focus group discussions reveals general agreement with the construct components as well as progress towards clarification over the indicator names. The findings from this analysis are key to our modified Delphi process as they provide evidence that the experts believed the construct was relevant to the profession and fit for purpose. This stakeholder confirmation was vital for the study to achieve before the WtE survey was launched for use with teachers and professional association members. Discussion of the indicators also reveals stakeholder awareness of the pressures being placed on the neophyte professionals through teaching standards, community expectations, and other stress points. The findings reveal the deep understanding education leaders have of the challenges ECTs face.

The first phase of the modified Delphi process has confirmed the Teacher Quality Construct as fit for purpose with industry stakeholders.

Synthesis of the data, both survey results and focus group discussions, validated the four components we adopted in our construct: intellectual, interpersonal, affective and intrapersonal. Furthermore, the stakeholders unequivocally endorsed all 37 research-derived indicators as being important for the teaching profession. We note that the identification by the expert panel of a subset of 12 essential indicators for ECTs represents a conceptualisation of teacher quality that is richly complex, holds high expectations of early career teachers and signals the need for ongoing support for them if they are to remain and thrive in the profession.

## Key References


Hanna, F., Oostdam, R., Severiens, S. E., & Zijlstra, B. J. H. (2019). Domains of teacher identity: A review of quantitative measurement instruments. *Educational Research Review*, *27*, 15–27. https://doi. org/10.1016/j.edurev.2019.01.003

Liu, K. (2015). Critical reflection as a framework for transformative learning in teacher education. *Educational Review*, *67*(2), 135–157. https:// doi.org/10.1080/00131911.2013.839546

Rowe, G., & Wright, G. (2011). The Delphi technique: Past, present, and future prospects – introduction to the special issue. *Technological Forecasting and Social Change*, *78*(9), 1487–1490. https://doi.org/10. 1016/j.techfore.2011.09.002

Santaguida, P., Dolovich, L., Oliver, D., Lamarche, L., Gilsing, A., Griffith, L. E., Richardson, J., Mangin, D., Kastner, M., & Raina, P. (2018). Protocol for a Delphi consensus exercise to identify a core set of criteria for selecting health related outcome measures (HROM) to be used in primary health care. *BMC Family Practice*, *19*, 1–14. https:// doi.org/10.1186/s12875-018-0831-5

# 5 Using modern measurement theory to test construct validity

*Jim Tognolini, Chris Freeman,
Alyson Simpson, and George Harb*

## Introduction

The teaching profession currently lacks a shared framework for identifying, measuring, and supporting components of teacher quality. One of the key objectives of the What's the Evidence (WtE) study was to produce a research-informed evidence base of indicators of teacher quality, valued and supported by a wide range of educational stakeholders. This chapter is a practical demonstration of how Rasch Theory (RT) (Bond et al., 2020; Bond & Fox, 2007) can be applied to measure how much 'teacher quality' (the construct) is present through assessing the components and associated indicators that best describe the construct. The RT approach was adopted because it is a measurement theory that can be used to govern the construction of measurement rubrics with the same properties as measurement devices in the physical sciences. It could be argued that because of the multifaceted nature of such a construct of teacher quality it is difficult, if not impossible to measure. However, the researchers were influenced by Lee Cronbach's (1990) argument that if something exists, it exists in some amount. If it exists in some amount, then it can be measured. Numerous reports discuss 'teacher quality' as something that exists in some amount (Stacey et al., 2019; Teng & Alonzo, 2023) and as such, it can be measured. In addition, the study was also driven by Hargreaves and Braun's (2013) challenge to start measuring things that are valued rather than only valuing things that can be measured. So, a measurement model was introduced to complement the iterative Delphi process that is described in Chapter 4.

This chapter loops back to the beginning of the first round of data collection to describe the first steps of setting up the construct, and then outlines the process of analysis undertaken from two rounds of data collection. The process shows how the Teacher Quality Construct was aligned with the components and the indicators that were identified as being

DOI: 10.4324/9781003542575-5

associated with the construct through the literature review. The purpose of the analysis phase of the study was two-fold;

1  To provide evidence to maximise confidence in the validity of the set of components and associated indicators used to generate the measure of teacher quality; and
2  To develop a measurement scale that can be used to measure teacher quality.

The Rasch model maps constructs onto linear continua, with equal units that can be adjusted from a set origin. In educational measurement, such linear continua have been called 'developmental continua', 'learning progressions', 'progress maps', 'construct maps' or 'road maps' when each unit represents a level of performance with descriptors of what students know and can do in relation to the construct observed (Bennett, 2018; Masters & Forster, 1996; Wilson, 2018). Tognolini (2018) defined measurement as the "process of assigning a number to a performance to represent a location with respect to the developmental continuum underlying the performance that indicates how much of the construct being assessed is present" (p. 2). A rubric built using the tenets of modern measurement theory is referred to as a measurement rubric. It is construct-oriented and focuses on describing an independent and unidimensional 'ruler' that could be used to locate teacher quality along a developmental continuum that represents the construct.

## Identifying the components and indicators of teacher quality

This chapter describes the preparatory processes needed to refine our definition of teacher quality and prioritise the indicators that fit our cultural context. First, Confirmatory Factor Analysis is used to refine and affirm the construct. Then the Rasch modelling process demonstrates an alternative representation of how construct confirmation can be achieved showing the relationship of the components and indicators to the construct and to each other. This work demonstrates statistically that the indicators to be used in the rubric were relevant to the construct.

As a result of the scoping review undertaken at the beginning of the WtE study, 37 indicators had been identified as relevant to the Teacher Quality Construct created by the researchers. These indicators were located within components as shown in Figure 1.1 of Chapter 1. The researchers then held focus groups with a purposive sample of educational stakeholders and asked them to rate each of the 37 indicators as to their importance (Essential, Very Desirable, Somewhat Desirable or Not

Relevant) in capturing the meaning of definitional aspects of teacher quality with respect to early career teachers (ECTs) in NSW, Australia. The stakeholder sample comprised representatives from leaders of national policy bodies, state-based education systems, teacher unions, professional associations, and teachers. This initial step provided the team of researchers with further confidence that the construct might be viable, yet at this stage the strength of the relationship of indicators to each other and the overall construct had not been tested.

The indicators had been grouped into four interwoven components: Intellectual, Interpersonal, Affective, and Intrapersonal qualities, using conceptual logic. The intent of the analysis reported in this chapter was to use Classical Test Theory (CTT) (Crocker & Algina, 1986; DeVellis, 2016; Murphy & Davidshofer, 2001) to provide evidence as to the integrity of the construct through exploratory and Confirmatory Factor Analysis and then use RT to produce measures of relative importance based on the ratings of the stakeholders. The question to be answered is whether the components and associated indicators can be considered to produce a unidimensional construct for the purpose of measurement using a measurement rubric. Unidimensionality is a requirement of measurement when the intention is to locate participants and questions on a single construct. This is true for all measurement in both the physical and social sciences. If one number is required to summarise location on the measurement rubric (scale), then it is considered unidimensional by the user of the rubric. This is analogous to threads being woven together to produce a rope or scores on different subjects being combined to produce a test score in the Programme for International Student Assessment (PISA).

The next section analyses the data collected from the stakeholder rating of the relative importance of each of the 37 indicators in capturing the construct of teacher quality.


### *Analysis 1: Stakeholder ratings*

In November of 2022, as part of the modified Delphi process a survey using a Likert scale structure was administered to a sample of currently serving primary and secondary school teachers and educational stakeholders in NSW, Australia. This yielded a total of 257 responses: educational experts (n = 16), educational leaders (n= 8) and teachers (n = 233). The survey presented participants with a list of 37 indicators of teacher quality, divided into four components - Intellectual, Interpersonal, Affective, and Intrapersonal. There are 10, 9, 9 and 9 indicators in each of the 4 components respectively. Each of the indicators was presented to the participants in the survey in a Likert format and rated as Essential, Very Desirable, Somewhat Desirable or Not Relevant.

*Table 5.1* Coding of the response

| Rating | Code | Mean response rating (MRR) |
|---|---|---|
| Essential | 4 | $M \geq 3.5$ |
| Very Desirable | 3 | $2.5 \leq M < 3.5$ |
| Somewhat Desirable | 2 | $1.5 \leq M < 2.5$ |
| Not Relevant | 1 | $M < 1.5$ |

Table 5.1 shows how the responses were coded. The column headed Mean Response Rating (MRR) shows the range of mean responses associated with each rating. For example, if the mean response (M) was equal to or greater than 3.5, the overall rating of the respondents was classified as Essential; if the mean rating was equal to or greater than 2.51 and less than 3.50, the overall rating was classified as Very Desirable, and so forth.

## Analyses conducted

Classical Test Theory (CTT) was conducted using the SPSS programme. It generated mean affirmation and correlation statistics between the indicators and among components.

### *Analysis outcomes*

*Analysis 1*

Table 5.2 shows the Indicator Number (I), Component (C), Indicator Name (N), Mean Response (M) and Mean Response Rating (MRR) which was based upon the mean response. For example, the indicator of Cognition within the component of Intellectual qualities had a mean of 3.63. As the M was greater than 3.5, the MRR was Essential. Similarly, Indicator Number 16 is Leadership which is located in the Interpersonal qualities component and has an M of 2.36 which gives it an MMR of Somewhat Desirable.

Table 5.2 shows that 19 indicators were rated as Essential; 17 were rated as Very Desirable; and 1 as Somewhat Desirable.

Given that the indicators were grounded in significant research it was not surprising to observe a high degree of agreement in the overall responses by the respondents. That is, there was only 1 indicator that had an overall rating of Somewhat Desirable. All the others were Essential or Very Desirable. The indicator that was the most essential in relation to teacher quality was Resilience (mean = 3.84).

*Table 5.2* Mean responses by indicator (SPSS) for Analysis 1

| Indicator number (I) | Component (C) | Indicator name (N) | Mean response (M) | Mean response rating (MRR) |
| --- | --- | --- | --- | --- |
| Q01 | Intellectual qualities | Cognition | 3.63 | Essential |
| Q02 | | Decision making | 3.45 | Very Desirable |
| Q03 | | Problem solving | 3.66 | Essential |
| Q04 | | Creativity | 3.17 | Very Desirable |
| Q05 | | Judgement | 3.45 | Very Desirable |
| Q06 | | Logic and reasoning | 3.44 | Very Desirable |
| Q07 | | Analytical | 3.24 | Very Desirable |
| Q08 | | Curiosity | 3.50 | Essential |
| Q09 | | Reflective practice | 3.72 | Essential |
| Q10 | | Beliefs and expectations | 3.32 | Very Desirable |
| Q11 | Interpersonal qualities | Agency | 2.84 | Very Desirable |
| Q12 | | Self-efficacy | 3.38 | Very Desirable |
| Q13 | | Motivation/commitment | 3.82 | Essential |
| Q14 | | Communication | 3.78 | Essential |
| Q15 | | Advocacy | 2.98 | Very Desirable |
| Q16 | | Leadership | 2.36 | Somewhat Desirable |
| Q17 | | Collaboration and relationship building | 3.64 | Essential |
| Q18 | | Influence | 2.62 | Very Desirable |
| Q19 | | Adaptability | 3.76 | Essential |
| Q20 | Affective qualities | Social and emotional intelligence | 3.60 | Essential |
| Q21 | | Cultural competence | 3.31 | Very Desirable |
| Q22 | | Collegiality | 3.59 | Essential |
| Q23 | | Empathetic | 3.59 | Essential |
| Q24 | | Negotiation and conflict management | 3.27 | Very Desirable |
| Q25 | | Social awareness | 3.54 | Essential |
| Q26 | | Respect for difference and diversity | 3.77 | Essential |
| Q27 | | Values and attitudes | 3.58 | Essential |
| Q28 | | Morals and ethics | 3.67 | Essential |
| Q29 | Intrapersonal qualities | Patience | 3.67 | Essential |
| Q30 | | Initiative | 3.30 | Very Desirable |
| Q31 | | Persistence | 3.66 | Essential |
| Q32 | | Resilience | 3.84 | Essential |
| Q33 | | Self-awareness | 3.44 | Very Desirable |
| Q34 | | Self-confidence | 3.19 | Very Desirable |
| Q35 | | Self-evaluation | 3.49 | Very Desirable |
| Q36 | | Self-discipline | 3.46 | Very Desirable |
| Q37 | | Time management | 3.59 | Essential |

A table similar in structure to Table 5.3 was prepared to show the research team the indicators that were considered least essential by the respondents. Table 5.3 shows the seven indicators that had the lowest M and had less than 40% of the respondents rating them as Essential. The table shows, for example, that Leadership had an M of 2.36 and was

*Table 5.3* Indicators with the lowest M who have also less than 40% of respondents rating them as Essential

| Indicator number(I) | Component(C) | Indicator name(N) | Mean response (M) | Percentage rated as less than 40% Essential |
| --- | --- | --- | --- | --- |
| Q16 | Interpersonal qualities | Leadership | 2.36 | 9.0% |
| Q18 | Interpersonal qualities | Influence | 2.62 | 14.0% |
| Q11 | Interpersonal qualities | Agency | 2.84 | 10.6% |
| Q15 | Interpersonal qualities | Advocacy | 2.98 | 29.6% |
| Q04 | Intellectual qualities | Creativity | 3.17 | 34.8% |
| Q34 | Intrapersonal qualities | Self-confidence | 3.19 | 34.9% |
| Q07 | Intellectual qualities | Analytical | 3.24 | 35.0% |

identified as being Essential by 9% of the respondents. The research team agreed that the response may have reflected some ambiguity in the minds of the respondents as to context of Leadership. It is not clear whether respondents were relating their ranking of leadership to appropriateness at school executive, disciplinary area, or classroom level.

As a Delphi process works towards consensus by "collecting and distilling knowledge from a group of experts by means of a series of questionnaires interspersed with controlled opinion feedback" (Millar et al., 2006, p. 7), the research team used the results of the first analysis to decide which indicators should progress to the second round of the survey. The reduction in the number of indicators to 30 was undertaken prior to the second round of data collection. The second round of data analysis was based on the 30 indicators remaining of the original 37.

*Analysis 2*

A total of 167 respondents returned the second survey. One hundred and fourteen respondents completed the surveys, including demographic data and ratings of each of the 30 remaining indicators of teacher quality. Forty-two respondents completed the demographic data but did not rate any of the indicators and 11 respondents rated some indicators, but not others. Table 5.4 shows the returned responses by Group (Experts, Leaders, and Teachers) and degree of completion (Complete; Partially Complete; No rating of Indicators).

IBM SPSS software was used in the same way as was conducted in Analysis 1.

SPSS ANALYSIS

Table 5.5 shows the mean rating for each indicator. These mean values show that the Group were very consistent in their ratings of the indicators

*Table 5.4* Responses by group for Analysis 2

| Group | Complete | Partially complete | No rating of indicators | Totals |
|---|---|---|---|---|
| Experts | 2 | 0 | 1 | 3 |
| Leaders | 5 | 0 | 0 | 5 |
| Teachers | 107 | 11 | 41 | 159 |
| **Composite data set** | **114** | **11** | **42** | **167** |

*Table 5.5* Mean response by indicator for Analysis 2

| Indicator number (I) | Component (C) | Indicator name (N) | Mean response (M) |
|---|---|---|---|
| 1 | Intellectual qualities | Cognition | 3.51 |
| 2 | | Decision making | 3.31 |
| 3 | | Problem solving | 3.51 |
| 4 | | Judgement | 3.37 |
| 5 | | Logic and reasoning | 3.46 |
| 6 | | Curiosity | 3.42 |
| 7 | | Reflective practice | 3.69 |
| 8 | | Beliefs and expectations | 3.36 |
| 9 | Interpersonal qualities | Self-efficacy | 3.30 |
| 10 | | Motivation/commitment | 3.72 |
| 11 | | Communication | 3.68 |
| 12 | | Collaboration and relationship building | 3.68 |
| 13 | | Adaptability | 3.68 |
| 14 | Affective qualities | Social and emotional intelligence | 3.54 |
| 15 | | Cultural competence | 3.30 |
| 16 | | Collegiality | 3.46 |
| 17 | | Empathetic | 3.38 |
| 18 | | Negotiation and conflict management | 3.19 |
| 19 | | Social awareness | 3.43 |
| 20 | | Respect for difference and diversity | 3.67 |
| 21 | | Values and attitudes | 3.49 |
| 22 | | Morals and ethics | 3.65 |
| 23 | Intrapersonal qualities | Patience | 3.53 |
| 24 | | Initiative | 3.32 |
| 25 | | Persistence | 3.62 |
| 26 | | Resilience | 3.78 |
| 27 | | Self-awareness | 3.51 |
| 28 | | Self-evaluation | 3.51 |
| 29 | | Self-discipline | 3.50 |
| 30 | | Time Management | 3.51 |

and were of the view that all 30 are significant contributors to their view of teacher quality for ECTs.


RELIABILITY

In the case of Likert scale surveys, Cronbach's alpha ($\alpha$) is generally used as a measure of the internal consistency of the indicators. This provides an indication of the extent to which the indicators measure the same construct (in this case, the construct of teacher quality and each of the 4 components that load onto teacher quality). Table 5.6 shows these reliabilities for all the indicators and then the indicators analysed by component.

As a 'rule of thumb' guide, reliability values above 0.7 are deemed 'acceptable,' above 0.8 'good,' and above 0.9 'excellent' as indicators of the internal consistency of a set of indicators (Taber, 2018). In all cases the reliability meets or exceeds the 'acceptable' value. These results confirmed that the 30 indicators are aligned with the construct of teacher quality (reliability = 0.91) and that there is a strong alignment between the indicators comprising each of the 4 components of teacher quality (reliabilities of 0.75, 0.73, 0.84 and 0.84 for Intellectual, Interpersonal, Affective and Intrapersonal qualities respectively).

Table 5.7 shows the responses by rating of the respondents for both analysis 1 and analysis 2.

Correlations are used to describe how two constructs, measures or variables are related to one another. They have the particular property that they can be descriptive and inferential at the same time. That is, they can describe data and infer a relationship from samples and populations (Wilson & Sloane, 2000). The relationship between the constructs is measured by a correlation coefficient (r). The numerical values for correlation coefficients range from $-1$ through to 0 through to $+1$, where $+1$ and $-1$ are perfect correlations, and they rarely occur in the real world. The r gives an indication of the strength and direction of the relationship between 2 constructs.

*Table 5.6* Reliabilities for the whole set of teacher quality indicators and for each of the 4 components

| *Components* | *Number of indicators* | *Reliabilities* |
| --- | --- | --- |
| All indicators | 30 | 0.91 |
| Intellectual qualities | 8 | 0.75 |
| Interpersonal qualities | 5 | 0.73 |
| Affective qualities | 9 | 0.84 |
| Intrapersonal qualities | 8 | 0.84 |

*Table 5.7* Response by rating for 30 indicators obtained from Analysis 1 and 2

| Indicator | Analysis 1 | | | | Analysis 2 | | | |
|---|---|---|---|---|---|---|---|---|
| | Essential | Very Desirable | Somewhat Desirable | Not Relevant | Essential | Very Desirable | Somewhat Desirable | Not Relevant |
| Cognition | 57.60% | 36.80% | 5.60% | 0.00% | 67.2% | 27.9% | 4.9% | 0.0% |
| Decision making | 42.40% | 48.80% | 8.00% | 0.80% | 53.4% | 36.8% | 9.8% | 0.0% |
| Problem solving | 56.00% | 39.20% | 4.80% | 0.00% | 71.4% | 23.3% | 4.9% | 0.5% |
| Judgement | 44.00% | 48.80% | 7.20% | 0.00% | 53.7% | 37.1% | 8.3% | 1.0% |
| Logic and reasoning | 51.20% | 45.60% | 3.20% | 0.00% | 49.3% | 44.4% | 6.3% | 0.0% |
| Curiosity | 54.40% | 33.60% | 11.20% | 0.80% | 59.5% | 30.7% | 8.8% | 1.0% |
| Reflective practice | 73.60% | 23.20% | 2.40% | 0.80% | 76.2% | 18.9% | 4.9% | 0.0% |
| Beliefs and expectations | 48.00% | 40.00% | 12.00% | 0.00% | 45.9% | 40.0% | 12.7% | 1.5% |
| Self-efficacy | 43.00% | 43.80% | 13.20% | 0.00% | 43.6% | 49.2% | 6.7% | 0.5% |
| Motivation/commitment | 75.20% | 22.30% | 2.50% | 0.00% | 81.5% | 18.0% | 0.5% | 0.0% |
| Communication | 71.10% | 25.60% | 3.30% | 0.00% | 79.0% | 19.0% | 2.1% | 0.0% |
| Collaboration and relationship building | 69.40% | 28.90% | 1.70% | 0.00% | 68.2% | 27.2% | 4.1% | 0.5% |
| Adaptability | 71.10% | 25.60% | 3.30% | 0.00% | 76.4% | 22.6% | 1.0% | 0.0% |
| Social and emotional intelligence | 57.10% | 39.50% | 3.40% | 0.00% | 62.8% | 34.0% | 2.6% | 0.5% |
| Cultural competence | 44.50% | 40.30% | 14.30% | 0.80% | 41.4% | 47.1% | 10.5% | 1.1% |
| Collegiality | 53.80% | 37.80% | 8.40% | 0.00% | 63.4% | 31.9% | 3.7% | 1.1% |
| Empathetic | 48.70% | 41.20% | 9.20% | 0.80% | 60.7% | 36.7% | 2.1% | 0.5% |
| Negotiation and conflict management | 34.50% | 50.40% | 15.10% | 0.00% | 37.7% | 49.2% | 13.1% | 0.0% |
| Social awareness | 52.90% | 37.00% | 9.20% | 0.80% | 58.1% | 36.7% | 5.2% | 0.0% |
| Respect for difference and diversity | 70.60% | 25.20% | 4.20% | 0.00% | 80.0% | 17.4% | 2.1% | 0.5% |
| Values and attitudes | 56.30% | 36.10% | 7.60% | 0.00% | 61.3% | 34.6% | 4.2% | 0.0% |
| Morals and ethics | 71.40% | 21.80% | 6.70% | 0.00% | 69.6% | 27.2% | 3.1% | 0.0% |
| Patience | 57.00% | 38.60% | 4.40% | 0.00% | 68.4% | 29.5% | 2.1% | 0.0% |
| Initiative | 43.90% | 44.70% | 11.40% | 0.00% | 43.2% | 42.6% | 13.2% | 1.1% |

| | | | | | | | |
|---|---|---|---|---|---|---|---|
| Persistence | 65.80% | 30.70% | 3.50% | 0.00% | 67.7% | 29.6% | 2.7% | 0.0% |
| Resilience | 80.70% | 16.70% | 2.60% | 0.00% | 86.3% | 11.1% | 2.6% | 0.0% |
| Self-awareness | 57.00% | 36.80% | 6.10% | 0.00% | 47.9% | 47.4% | 4.2% | 0.5% |
| Self-evaluation | 55.30% | 40.40% | 4.40% | 0.00% | 52.4% | 43.4% | 4.2% | 0.0% |
| Self-discipline | 57.00% | 36.00% | 7.00% | 0.00% | 52.1% | 41.1% | 6.3% | 0.5% |
| Time management | 57.90% | 35.10% | 7.00% | 0.00% | 64.2% | 30.0% | 5.8% | 0.0% |

The researchers used Confirmatory Factor Analysis (CFA) (Rogers, 2024b) to assess the extent to which the background work of identifying the indicators that load onto a single construct (teacher quality) is appropriate. CFA is a popular CTT data analysis procedure in the social sciences because it addresses theoretical models where the construct is difficult to measure. In this case CFA is used to determine how well each of the 30 indicators relates to the construct of teacher quality; and a second CFA shows how each of the indicators relates to the 4 components to which they have been assigned by the researchers.

Figure 5.1 shows the correlations between the indicators and the single construct of teacher quality.

It can be seen from Figure 5.1 that the indicators that were most highly, positively correlated with the construct of teacher quality are Self-discipline (.70), Self-awareness (0.64), Empathy (0.62), Communication (0.57), Social and emotional intelligence (0.57), and Values and attitudes (0.57). The indicators that were less correlated, although still positively correlated, are Patience (0.32), Decision making (0.34), Problem solving (0.35) and Cognition (0.37). What the data imply is that measures of the indicators will contribute to a measure of the Teacher Quality Construct, and that some will contribute more than others.

Figure 5.2 shows the relationship between the indicators and their a-priori alignment with a component and the relationships between components.

From Figure 5.2, the greatest correlation exists between the Intelligence qualities and the Affective qualities (0.70). It can also be seen that the range of correlations among the components is small, which implies that they do relate to a common construct.


## Discussion

The CTT analysis presented in this chapter has focused on converting responses obtained from a Likert questionnaire asking respondents to rate the importance of 30 indicators as measures of teacher quality for ECTs. The results suggest that the 30 indicators do load onto a single measure, which is the construct the researchers a priori have defined as teacher quality. The intention in the future is to develop measures of each of the indicators and have teachers complete these measures. The results on those measures will provide the location on a measurement scale developed to measure teacher quality. This is analogous to measuring mathematics in the cognitive domain (Shepard et al., 2018). Students can sit for sub-tests in number, space, and measurement and because they all load onto the broad construct of mathematics, the results on these tests can be used to measure performance on mathematics.

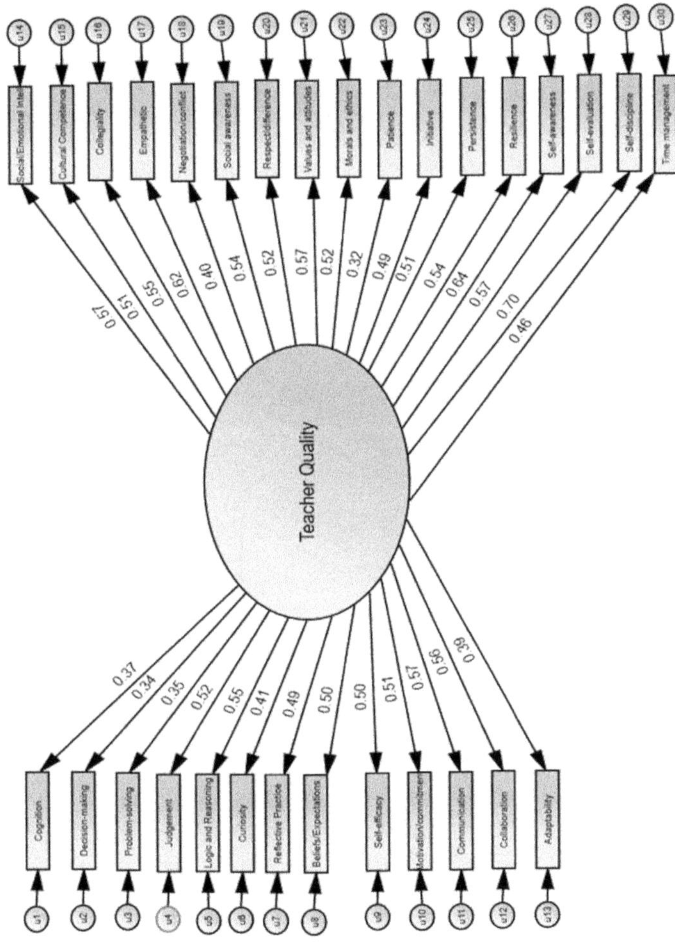

*Figure 5.1* Correlations between the 30 indicators and the Teacher Quality Construct.

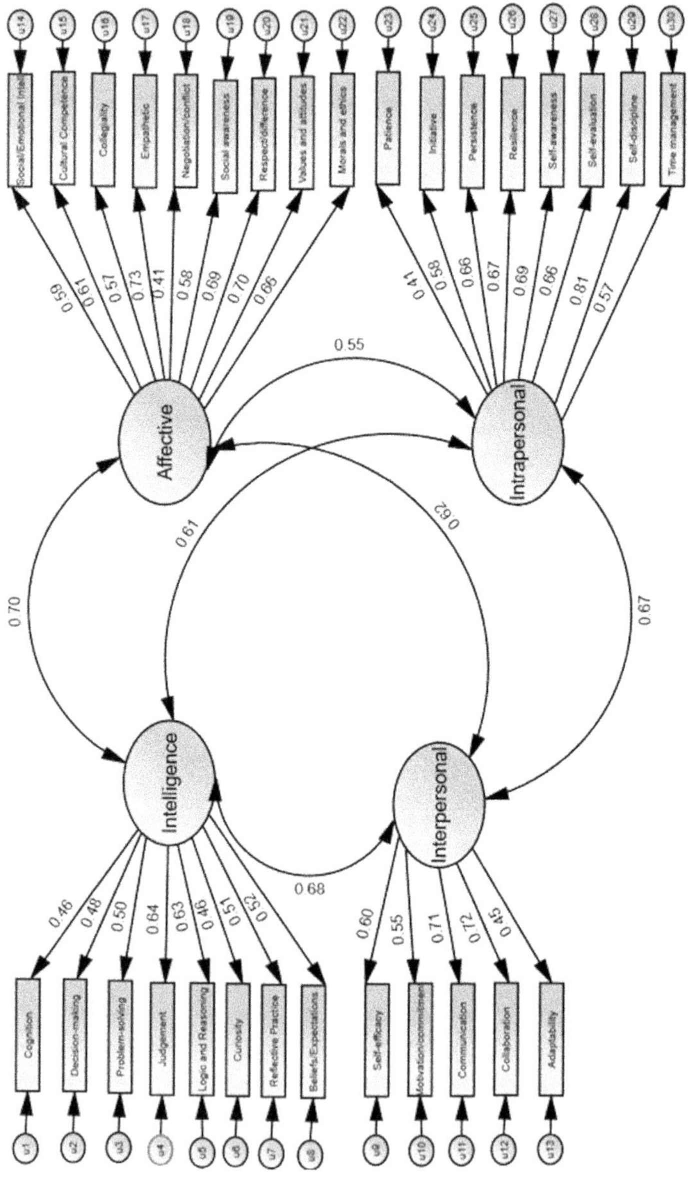


*Figure 5.2* Correlations among the components and between each of the components and related indicators

As stated earlier in the chapter, RT is used as a step towards building a measurement scale for measuring how much of the Teacher Quality Construct is present, based upon responses to the indicator measures. As with measurement in the physical sciences, the Rasch Model locates respondents (teachers) and indicator measures on the same scale. The analysis presented in this chapter demonstrates how RT could have been used to analyse the Likert questionnaire instead of using CTT. Both analytic tools have helped to confirm the fit of the indicators to the construct.

### Rasch theory analysis using RUMM 2030

Table 5.8 shows the relative difficulty of the indicators from easiest to hardest in the column headed 'Rasch Difficulty' (R). The more negative the measure of difficulty, the easier it is for the respondents to agree with; the more positive, the more teacher quality the respondents must have to agree with it.

For example, in Table 5.8, the indicator of Decision making has a location (difficulty) of 1.947. This is the largest positive R and as such, it means that respondents found this indicator the most challenging indicator to agree with as a measure of teacher quality. Another way to say this is that respondents believed that a teacher must have a 'lot' of teacher quality to agree that Decision making is a necessary characteristic of quality teachers. Conversely, the respondents suggested that Motivation/commitment with a R of −0.887 was considered relatively easy for respondents to rate as an indicator of teacher quality.

Table 5.8 also provides a summary of the fit of the various indicators to the requirements of RT. It is obtained from the analysis of all responses and provides a mechanism for identifying any indicators that might not accord with the expectations of RT. The column headed 'Fit Residual' (F) in Table 5.8 is the most relevant for measuring fit to the Rasch Model, informed by RT. This column indicates the extent to which the responses of the participants accord with what is expected by RT.

It can be noticed from Table 5.8 that the F for all indicators lies within the range $-2.5 < F < 2.5$, which indicates that the indicators fit the Rasch model. This also implies that they are measuring the same construct (teacher quality) and that the scale is relatively unidimensional.

It can be seen from Table 5.8 that the indicator that had the biggest positive F was Patience (F = 2.159). This suggests that the respondents who were most positive in rating the indicators, were less positive on the indicator of Patience than RT expected, or predicted, based upon their ratings on the other indicators. Conversely the respondents who rated the indicators less important, rated Patience higher than expected. The F for Motivation/commitment (F = −0.937) on the other hand suggests that

*Table 5.8* Location and fit residual for all indicators

| Indicator number(I) | Component(C) | Indicator name(IN) | Rasch difficulty(R) | Fit residual(F) |
|---|---|---|---|---|
| 1 | Intellectual qualities | Cognition | −0.317 | 1.589 |
| 2 | | Decision making | 1.947 | 1.554 |
| 3 | | Problem solving | −0.149 | 0.597 |
| 4 | | Judgement | −0.242 | 0.294 |
| 5 | | Logic and reasoning | −0.429 | −0.476 |
| 6 | | Curiosity | 1.746 | 1.388 |
| 7 | | Reflective practice | 1.079 | −0.321 |
| 8 | | Beliefs and expectations | −0.186 | 0.365 |
| 9 | Interpersonal qualities | Self-efficacy | −0.101 | 1.344 |
| 10 | | Motivation/ commitment | −0.887 | −0.937 |
| 11 | | Communication | −0.575 | −1.362 |
| 12 | | Collaboration and relationship building | −0.532 | −1.260 |
| 13 | | Adaptability | −0.654 | −0.173 |
| 14 | Affective qualities | Social and emotional intelligence | −0.396 | −1.086 |
| 15 | | Cultural competence | 1.699 | 0.534 |
| 16 | | Collegiality | −0.330 | −0.127 |
| 17 | | Empathetic | 1.524 | −0.724 |
| 18 | | Negotiation and conflict management | 0.027 | 1.468 |
| 19 | | Social awareness | 1.700 | −0.552 |
| 20 | | Respect for difference and diversity | −0.645 | −0.861 |
| 21 | | Values and attitudes | −0.350 | −1.064 |
| 22 | | Morals and ethics | −0.446 | −0.763 |
| 23 | Intrapersonal qualities | Patience | −0.225 | 2.159 |
| 24 | | Initiative | −0.174 | 0.765 |
| 25 | | Persistence | −0.622 | −0.450 |
| 26 | | Resilience | −0.796 | −1.010 |
| 27 | | Self-awareness | −0.443 | −0.939 |
| 28 | | Self-evaluation | −0.497 | −0.023 |
| 29 | | Self-discipline | −0.495 | −1.762 |
| 30 | | Time management | −0.228 | 0.283 |

the respondents who were most positive overall on the ratings, were more positive about Motivation/commitment than what had been expected from the Rasch model; and, the respondents who were lower overall were less positive than expected from the Rasch model.

Figures 5.3 and 5.4 present examples of an Item Characteristic Curve (ICC) in RT. They demonstrate the effect of F for two indicators, Morals and ethics and Self-discipline. Both have relatively small, negative F of –0.763 and –1.762, respectively.

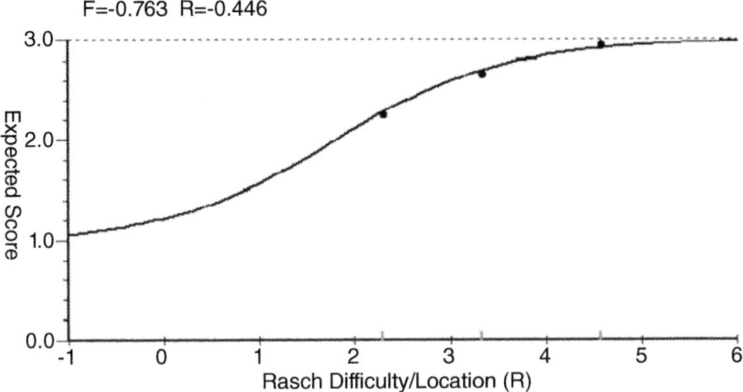


*Figure 5.3* Item Characteristic Curve (ICC) for Morals and ethics

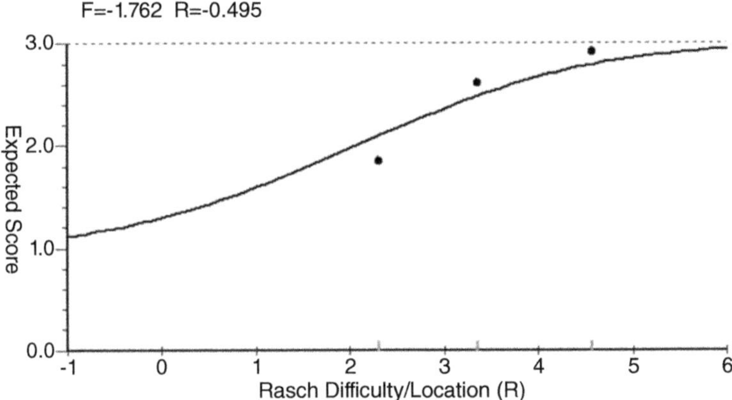


*Figure 5.4* Item Characteristic Curve (ICC) for Self-discipline

In the Figures, the line represents the expected scores based on RT. The dots show the actual scores obtained by three groups of respondents clustered by their overall score on the Likert questionnaire. One of the features of RT is that the scores of the respondents and the relative difficulties of the indicators are on the same scale. Figure 5.3 shows that the expected score and the actual score are close, as suggested by the small negative F.

By comparison, in Figure 5.4 there is a variation in between the expected scores (represented by the line) and the actual scores (represented by the dots). The dot corresponding to the most positive respondents (the dot furthest to the right) is above what RT expected, hence the respondents who were most positive overall were even more positive about this indicator than would have been expected based upon their responses to the overall survey. Similarly, the group of the respondents who were less positive overall were less positive than expected on this indicator. This raises the question as to why this response occurred.

## Conclusion

These paired statistical modelling tools provide evidence to support the contention that the 30 indicators identified by the researchers function uniformly to define the Teacher Quality Construct for early career teachers, and can contribute to the development of a measurement scale of teacher quality which can be used to generate evidence of the relationship between the construct and alternate measures of teacher effectiveness and quality, like Teaching Performance Assessments (TPAs).

As mentioned, these values should be considered with caution due to the sample size of this phase of the study. However, it should be noted that these curves show exceptional compliance to the expected model and would be considered well within the bounds of a unidimensional model.

In addition, it is stressed that this example has been carried out to demonstrate how RT can be applied to Likert questionnaires to produce measurement scales that enable respondents and the indicators that comprise the components that contribute to the underlying construct to be directly compared (Bennett, 2015). Further examination of RT and how a measurement scale for teacher quality can be generated will be discussed in Chapter 7.

## Key References

Bennett, R. E. (2018). Educational assessment: What to watch in a rapidly changing world. *Educational Measurement: Issues and Practice, 37*(4), 7–15. https://doi.org/10.1111/emip.12231

DeVellis, R. F. (2016). *Scale development: Theory and applications*. Sage Publications.

Shepard, L. A., Penuel, W. R., & Pellegrino, J. W. (2018). Using learning and motivation theories to coherently link formative assessment, grading practices, and large-scale assessment. *Educational Measurement: Issues and Practice, 37*(1), 21–34. https://doi.org/10.1111/emip.12189

Taber, K.S. (2018). The use of Cronbach's Alpha when developing and reporting research instruments in science education. *Research in Science Education, 48*, 1273–1296. https://doi.org/10.1007/s11165-016-9602-2

Wilson, M. (2018). Making measurement important for education: The crucial role of classroom assessment. *Educational Measurement: Issues and Practice, 37*(1), 5–20. https://doi.org/10.1111/emip.12188

# 6 What does it mean for early career teachers to be classroom ready?

*Rachel White, Alyson Simpson, Damian Maher, and George Harb*

## Introduction

It could be argued that there is no more contentious, complex, and uncertain period in a teacher's career than the early career stage. A teacher can be considered an early career teacher (ECT) during and up to the first five years of their career (Admiraal et al., 2023), as they are navigating employment opportunities, interactions with colleagues and students, and in some contexts working towards professional accreditation as they understand the social and cultural expectations of their teacher role. It is also a period of time where teachers are making the transition from pre-service to in-service, letting go of their 'student' identity and developing their 'teacher' identity (Ludecke & Cooper, 2023). This navigation of identity and role presents its own difficulties, as ECTs move from artificially constructed and externally dictated teaching environments curated during their pre-service learning, into the start of a career now determined by their own choices about community and practice (Beauchamp & Thomas, 2011).

A problematic issue that sits at the heart of that transition into the profession is the notion that pre-service teachers (PSTs) are 'classroom ready' at point of graduation. This term gained traction in international education policy and practice, primarily in Australia after a federal government report into initial teacher education (Craven et al., 2014) but also in other contexts such as the United Kingdom and Canada (Mayer et al., 2021) as education sectors explored how to best prepare pre-service teachers for what the profession expects. The denotative meaning of the term refers to how ready a teacher is to teach in a classroom and could be considered to be the "destination of initial teacher education" (Mayer et al., 2021, p. 218). According to the Craven et al. (2014), ECTs should be ready for the "rigour and challenges" of teaching (p. 3), which suggests a competency basis for assessing beginning teachers. However, the connotative meaning is more complex with research arguing that 'readiness for the

DOI: 10.4324/9781003542575-6

profession' (Sachs, 2000; Ingvarson et al., 2014) may be a more apt term, perceiving readiness as a 'milestone' in teacher career trajectory, rather than a benchmark (Alexander, 2018). This interpretation allows for complexity across teaching contexts and the need for ECTs to develop expertise over time.

Readiness can be interpreted as a teacher's level of preparedness as viewed through policy and expectations imposed on ECTs by others. However, it can also be viewed through a personal identity lens as ECTs own "expectations of success" (Haag & Megowan-Romanowicz, 2015, p. 420) as they commence engagement in teaching practice. This state of preparedness reflects an optimal level of professional competences, knowledges, practice, and engagement, acquired to a degree that allows them to effectively engage in the required work of teaching (Manasia et al., 2020; Mohamed et al., 2017). It can be linked to perceptions of self-efficacy (Howard et al., 2021), or the individual's belief in their ability to meet the challenges they may face. These views of classroom readiness imply that it is a concept that can be measured, or monitored, both internally and externally, linking it to both ECT identity as well as their capacity to enact their professional role.

The divergent conceptualisations of classroom readiness, as a milestone or benchmark in the beginning stages of a teacher's career, indicates that ECTs face conceptual tensions. They are seeking to create an identity that is malleable and sustainable (Morrison, 2013) while also contending with rigid definitions of professional standards, and a range of long held social, cultural, and collegial perceptions of who they are and what they should be expected to do. A teacher's readiness for the classroom, along with their identity as a teacher, is formed through self-perception and social interactions (Cooper & Olson, 1996), where "particular situations evoke particular parts of the self" (Akkerman & Meijer, 2011, p. 312). It is in the classroom where "graduate teachers often experience disjuncture from the world of teaching advocated elsewhere", and why these spaces can become places of "overwhelm, loneliness, isolation, and confusion for graduate teachers" (Stewart et al., 2021, p. 319). Teacher readiness benefits from the acquisition of knowledges and skills, but the research indicates teachers also need qualities such as self-management, commitment, adaptability, integrity, and motivation to be best prepared for the professional challenges that await them (Haag & Megowan-Romanowicz, 2015; Manasia et al., 2020; Mohamed et al., 2017). This confluence of teacher qualities, implemented in a supportive context, can allow all teachers to construct a more sustainable classroom ready identity and professional role.

This chapter discusses how a sample of Australian teacher perceptions about ECT qualities reflect a lack of agreement concerning the competencies and capacities needed for ECTs to engage effectively in the work of teaching. Our data analysis revealed interesting, varying perspectives on the attributes, capacities, and behaviours expected of ECTs, raising questions about the implications arising from the lack of consistency of definitions of classroom readiness currently adopted in policy and by classroom teachers. Although the data sample is small, the conceptual differences it reveals between those who see readiness as being ready to teach and those who see it as being ready for the profession are great. Understanding "the dissonances between the divergent conceptions of readiness in the educational community" (Alexander, 2018, p. 106) that ECTs must negotiate may provide insight to why some ECTs thrive while others just survive (Beltmann et al., 2011). For this reason, the chapter explores not only the ways in which the data reveals expectations of ECTs but also how these expectations have consequences for the formation of their future teacher identity.

## Methodology

The data and findings under discussion in this chapter were collected as part of the second round of the Delphi process undertaken by the WtE team, with the intent of confirming the indicators of teacher quality that could be considered 'essential' for ECTs. The first round of the Delphi process, described in Chapters 4 and 5, utilised focus groups and an online Qualtrics survey to gather perspectives on the 37 research-informed indicators of teacher quality initially identified as belonging to the Teacher Quality Construct. As a result of this initial round of data collection and analysis, seven indicators of teacher quality were removed for the round two survey as they had been determined to be 'least essential' for ECTs by the respondents of the first survey. These indicators were:

- Intellectual
  - Analytical: The ways in which teachers consider, analyse, and synthesise information.
  - Creativity: Inventiveness and innovation in how teachers approach or conceive of teaching.
- Interpersonal
  - Advocacy: A teacher's ability to be supportive and empowering of others.
  - Agency: A teacher's capacity to produce and affect actions.
  - Influence: The ways in which teachers can impact their context.
  - Leadership: How a teacher conceives of and asserts authority in a given context.
- Intrapersonal
  - Self-confidence: A teacher's trust in their own thoughts and behaviour.

Additionally, two indicators in the Affective component (Morals and ethics, and Values and attitudes) were identified as being considered similar to each other by respondents to the first survey, but were still both determined to be 'essential' for ECTs. These indicators were not removed from consideration or changed for the second iteration of the survey and, as such, responses for this component were not part of the data analysis.

In the second step of the Delphi process, another Qualtrics survey was engaged with by 165 educators in New South Wales (NSW). However, not all participants who commenced the survey completed it. A total of 114 participants completed the full survey. This second iteration of the survey took the same format as the first, asking participants to rank the listed indicators of teacher quality from 'most essential' to 'least essential'. However, in this iteration the seven indicators identified as 'least essential' in the first round had been removed for consideration. To allow participants to comment on the removal of the seven indicators, an additional, optional open-text question was added to the end of each component of the survey. For the components where indicators had been removed for the round 2 survey, participants were informed of the indicators that had been removed, provided with definitions of each indicator, and then asked the following question:

> Do you agree that they are not essential for early career teachers? If so why? OR, if you think they should be put back in, why do you believe they should have been included?

The analysis conducted for this chapter focused on the qualitative responses to these questions provided by the survey participants.

### *Coding*

The two lead authors undertook a comprehensive coding process of the qualitative responses. The data was first prepared for analysis by removing all irrelevant information created by the transfer of data from Qualtrics into Excel, creating pseudonyms for all respondents, and separating the data into responses related to the indicators removed from the Intellectual, Interpersonal, and Intrapersonal components. Each response was then broadly coded as Essential, Not Essential, or Ambiguous. A third of all response types were double coded, returning an alignment of 90%, rising to 100% after discussion about the remaining contentious codes (Table 6.1).

The Essential and Not Essential responses were then open and axial coded separately by the two lead authors, with procedural guidance for analysis provided by the lead author. The open coding process requires researchers to identify "distinct concepts and themes" in qualitative data (Williams & Moser, 2019, p. 48). Both researchers identified 140 open

*Table 6.1* Response type definitions

| | |
|---|---|
| **Essential** | The response specifies that one or more indicators are essential for ECTs. This may be phrased as 'essential', 'required', 'put back in', 'needed', 'crucial', 'imperative', 'critical', 'vital', 'important', 'necessary'. |
| **Not Essential** | The response specifies that one or more indicators are not essential for ECTs. This can include responses where the participant indicates one or more indicators may be *desirable*, but not essential. |
| **Ambiguous** | The response is unclear about whether one or more indicators should be considered essential for ECTs. This could include responses where the participant states that one indicator is essential, but another is not. |

codes combined. These were then axial coded by grouping open codes into broader categories (Cascio et al., 2019) representing a similar, overarching theme, in an effort to explore the different relationships between perspectives and what they might reveal about broader, more abstract phenomena (Scott et al., 2017). For example, responses coded as Understanding students, Teach students, Engage students, and Support students were grouped into the axial code Working with students. Appropriate Ambiguous responses (i.e. responses that contained perspectives that could be considered Essential and Not Essential) were open and axial coded by both researchers together. Both sets of axial codes were then selectively coded to identify common coding between the two lead researchers, and "cohesive and meaning-filled" overarching themes (Williams & Moser, 2019, p. 52).

## Results and discussion

Six broad themes were identified in the selective coding process, collated into three overarching areas for discussion as shown in Table 6.2. Some responses were connected to multiple selective codes. For example, when asked to consider whether self-confidence is essential for ECTs, T78 said, "Confidence comes with time and mastery. Not many are confident at the beginning and those who are, tend to be not so great", leading to this response being coded to the Career development and Self-confidence axial codes. It is worth noting that around 15% of all responses were coded as simply Essential or Not Essential as they provided no further explanation (eg. T43 responded to all questions with "They are very important" or "They are vital") and 14% of responses were not included for analysis as it was not possible to determine whether they believed the indicators in question were essential or not. For example, when asked to consider the quality of self-confidence, T97 responded, "I feel that all of

*Table 6.2* Definitions of the six identified overarching themes for discussion

| Theme | Definition |
| --- | --- |
| **ECT development** | Responses describing how indicators may be essential or not essential at different **career stages**, including the negative consequences of **self-confidence** and how **mentoring** can impact quality development. |
| **Teaching as cerebral or craft** | Responses describing the **intellectual challenge** inherent in teaching, or describing **teaching as a craft**, and/or the value of establishing the basics of practice. |
| **Interrelated qualities** | Responses describing how the indicators deemed 'least essential' for ECTs may **support other indicators** of teacher quality. |

the values above can be nurtured or squashed, depending on the environment the early career teacher is in".

The sections below discuss the three overarching themes emerging from analysis of the data collected from the open field responses of participants as noted above. The theme of ECT development is the umbrella heading under which discussion of the sub-themes of mentoring and self-confidence can be found. The theme of teaching as cerebral or craft is used as the heading under which discussion of contrasting perceptions of early career teaching as an intellectual challenge or an opportunity to hone a craft is completed. The third overarching theme relates to how participants recognised that qualities across and within the Teacher Quality Construct were interrelated. Under each heading we introduce the theme by positioning it in a body of relevant literature as well as provide a brief summary of the issues that arose using quotes from the survey. As we discuss the results, we note how points related to classroom readiness and/or teacher identity arise.

### Early career teacher development

Career development for teachers in general has been studied by scholars who have explored pressures on retention, support structures that contribute to career sustainability, and other topics (Admiraal et al., 2023; Day, 2017; Simpson et al., 2022). Commentary from participants in the WtE study portrays a complex view of ECT development, acknowledging that "beginners do not need to be experts" (Alexander, 2018, p. 110), but providing different perspectives on what qualities and aspects of practice should be prioritised in the early career period. There was variation around both *which* indicators were selected to be necessary and *when* they were deemed to be necessary. This view expects teacher quality will be developed in an ongoing process, where some qualities are judged to be more essential than others in different career stages.

Examining the rationales for which indicators were considered essential to a teacher's career development, a number of different underlying perspectives were presented. Some argued the removed indicators were essential for teachers at all stages of their career. For example, the intellectual qualities (creativity and analytical) were particularly considered to be core aspects of teachers work, necessary to develop a "strong foundation" (T3) and required "right from the get go" (T73). Others argued that the removed qualities were necessary for teachers to stay in teaching. Respondents stated that "creativity is essential to thrive as a teacher long term" (T36), "self-confidence is vital for survival in the early years" (T40), and that the four interpersonal qualities were necessary for ECTs "to ensure sustainability of the teaching profession" (T97). However, not all respondents agreed with this stance, with two respondents commenting that the removed qualities would not "help a newby survive" (T104), let alone maintain a commitment to the career.

Emerging strongly in these data was agreement that the removed indicators in particular were not essential for ECTs as they could be developed in due course. Sometimes this opinion was couched as a vague statement about the quality's 'development' or 'growth' over time. Others indicated the time factor by noting that the intellectual and interpersonal qualities would become more important at a later stage in a teacher's career. However, a group of participants commented that the indicators would be developed as teachers undertook the work and practice of teaching, implying these qualities were not necessary for beginning teachers as they could be learned on the job. T18 said that teachers can develop analytical capacities as they work with a mentor "to help guide through the mass of paperwork now required". Self-confidence can be developed as teachers experience "success and failures" (T66), or after they "perfect the craft of teaching" (T33). The interpersonal qualities can be developed as "a teacher progresses through their career" (T58), with "experience in the job and with opportunities provided by other leaders within the school community" (T39). These specific examples of the impact of the experience of teaching yielding development were few and far between.

With regard to factors that impact ECT professional development, the role of the mentor is key as it has the dual potential to "improve the performance and retention of beginning teachers" (Ingersoll & Strong, 2011, p. 4). For ECTs this support is vital as mentoring can help them develop the skills of teaching as well as confidence in their personal identity as teachers (Beijaard & Meijer, 2017). The commentary about mentoring emerged as a strong theme demonstrating that teachers think ECTs need support when they are starting out so that they can develop their skills over time with less pressure on them to be experts - "some of our ECTs don't know what they don't know and through mentoring and guidance will be able to develop these skills" (T79). The data highlight the recognition teachers have that working in a school environment can be a challenge for an ECT who deserve support. However, it is interesting to note that the need for ECTs to have expert mentoring in foundational competencies and skills was called out in particular, with T60 stating, "Early career teachers need to go into schools and learn from those that have had many years of experience, taking the best of well-practiced knowledge and applying it with new learning to better improve their teaching".

A small amount of commentary acknowledged the relational work of teachers noting that ECTs need mentors to help them build their confidence, such as "having a mentor teacher to help with assuring early career teachers- it's OK, you have got this, you are doing the right thing" (T18). As interpersonal factors such as managing collegial relationships have been identified as key to ECTs retention (Fetherston & Lummis, 2012), more emphasis could be paid to this aspect of mentoring. Overall, it was suggested that good mentors can take the weight off ECTs shoulders so they can attempt difficult tasks and take risks without the responsibility of working alone. In principle this is a sound recommendation and induction programs are embedded into schools as a result. However, not all schools have well-resourced mentoring programs so the efficacy of induction may depend on the school setting, creating inequity for ECTs in their early years of employment (Ingersoll & Strong, 2011; Schuck et al., 2018).

The comments on mentoring are largely expressed in positive tones recognising that ECTs need time to develop. However, a few negative comments suggest that ECTs who try to bring new knowledge to schools will not be well received as they do not have years of experience to understand that "what is theoretically right, does not sit well in practice" (T60). The general perception seems to be that "learning from others would be a better aim in early career" (T28). It is clear that "ECTs face different challenges as their teaching experience levels increase" (Black et al., 2023, p. 1) with Admiraal and Kittelsen Røberg (2023) noting that ECTs need support to develop and sustain their sense of self-efficacy in teaching. These opinions demonstrate the tensions ECTs face as they navigate colleagues' expectations of them in their role as teacher while they are seeking confirmation of their personal authenticity as a teacher who can contribute to the school community (Howard et al., 2021).

Self-confidence, as a general trait, refers to a person's trust in their own thoughts, behaviour, and abilities (Oney & Oksuzoglu-Guven, 2015), which can allow for someone to engage in independent work without constant reliance on others for guidance and advice. It is a quality that teachers can bring to the classroom from the beginning of their career, as well as something that can be developed over time. However, a concern expressed by some teachers in these data was related to ECTs having *too much* self-confidence. The challenge according to the respondents was that if ECTs trusted their own knowledge and experience over that of more experienced colleagues, their personal growth would be stunted. Though some respondents did consider it essential for ECTs, the vast majority agreed it was not, and a subset of participants seemed to view 'self-confidence' as a short step away from arrogance, a lack of humility, and an unwillingness to accept feedback or support. Too much self-confidence could lead to ECTs "accepting no help, support or advice" (T12), having "a closed mind" (T47), make ECTs "hard to guide and support to develop their practices" (T86) and "have a high opinion of themselves" (T76). Several respondents also specifically commented on self-confidence impacting an ECT's capacity to reflect, making them less open to genuine self-reflection. Despite the view that opportunities to reflect on their teaching strategies help ECTs to recognise their potential which build self-confidence (T30), one respondent commented, "The less self confidence, especially early on, the better" (T17).

These responses speak to the fine line that ECTs often have to tread when they are entering a school as a new teacher, especially early on when they have comparatively less experience and lack the contextual knowledge other colleagues have. One of the ECT respondents explained that, "Usually when you're a first year teacher and you come with a lot of confidence, that can be perceived [as] that you are unwilling to learn because you already know everything. Not necessary a good mindset to start your career with" (T70). It could be suggested that participants wrongly read ECTs as over-confident when they are expressing the buoyant naivety created by the knowledge and support inculcated in initial teacher education. In a study of confidence levels Keese et al. (2022) demonstrated that early experience in school teaching and the practical reality of the classroom led to a decrease in confidence for ECTs as they came to terms with the complexity of teaching. The survey responses lead to interesting questions about what levels of self-confidence are appropriate for ECTs to be classroom ready, and how to gauge whether an ECT needs self-confidence to maintain their identity as a teacher in balance with their ability to grow and develop into their role.

### Teaching as cerebral or a craft

There is a long-standing debate on the status of teaching as an intellectual profession (Beauchamp, et al., 2015; Eisner, 1979; Shulman, 1986; Stacey et al., 2019). Some argue it can be represented through competencies and skills as a "craft" that as Eisner notes depends on mastery of "routine and repertoire" (Eisner. 1979, p.10). A complementary view of teaching frames it as reliant on the individual who can undertake "knowledge-informed intellectual work involving professional decisions in relation to student learning" (Stacey et al., 2019, p. 10). Both these two contrasting perspectives on the nature of teaching were represented in these data. Comments about teaching as a craft were only prevalent where respondents affirmed the nature of the seven listed indicators as non-essential, whereas comments that positioned teaching as an intellectual practice appeared where participants rated the removed indicators as essential. Quotes taken from the data clearly illustrate the tension existing between perceptions of teaching as a craft or as an intellectual profession.

The craft of teaching view represents the ECT phase as a time for junior colleagues to master competencies and follow standards that will lead to them successfully fulfilling the role of teaching (Beauchamp et al., 2015). As the craft of teaching is associated with prescribed curriculum interpretation, ECTs are expected to follow instructional routines (Hordern et al., 2021). The research suggests this perception risks backgrounding "the intellectual underpinnings of teachers' work, that underplay its profoundly emotional and social dimensions" (Connell, 2009, p. 220). Yet the view of teaching as "a predefined set of skills or practices that make up the craft" (Alexander, 2018, p.106) to be mastered comes through clearly in the commentary. Respondents speak about teaching for ECTs as a matter of mastering the practice of basic skills so they can "just get their job done" (T62). This reductionist view of teaching emphasises ECTs' responsibility to follow guidelines or procedures demonstrating "an understanding of teaching as essentially a craft rather than an intellectual activity" (McNamara & Murray, 2013, p. 22). The opinions expressed are a mix of the need to support ECTs so they avoid making mistakes while they are deepening their teaching experience - "teachers just need to follow the procedure" (T34), "early careers teachers need to focus on evidence based practice, understanding the curriculum and how to teach it" (T74) - as well as comments that show a lack of trust for ECTs who should not attempt to "put their own spin on teaching" (T19) and "in the early years of teaching, early career teachers need to follow the basics to ensure they are teaching what is required" (T18).

In contrast, responses conceptualising teaching as intellectual challenge emphasise the importance of ECTs being empowered to act as "deliberative, intellectual professionals" (Simpson et al., 2022, p. 10) who can "think on their feet" (T23, T92) to respond to the dynamics of contextual factors. This view proposes the critical importance of ECTs basing their decisions on "analysis and synthesis of information" (T96) so they can "go with the flow in the classroom and feel licensed to allow the lesson to develop elsewhere than originally planned" (T105). In contrast to the craft views, respondents suggested ECTs should be independent thinkers who are able to "take risks" (T79), "think beyond the prescriptive approach to lesson presentation" (T47) and "create learning experiences suitable for student needs, rather than teach from standard units of work that may not cater for all" (T77). It was also acknowledged that ECTs need to balance their self-confidence with "their ability to listen, to reflect honestly and deeply on their teaching performance and to be willing to take and/or seek advice" (T30). Most of the comments in support of this view were recorded in response to the removal of intellectual indicators. However, additional comments on the removal of the interpersonal indicators also note the intellectual nature of teaching because ultimately ECTs are individuals who work in the role as teachers but need to take personal "responsibility for their own professional learning" (T25) to "connect, engage and educate their students effectively" (T26) and "think beyond the prescriptive approach to lesson presentation" (T17). These comments align with the view that "teaching as a profession makes room for a multiplicity of conceptions of teaching and actively promotes knowledge and practice across this range of possibilities in the identification and assessment of readiness" (Alexander, 2018, p. 106).

### Interrelated qualities

Thus far, these data have been discussed in relation to overarching themes that encompass the contrasting epistemological views of teaching that exist as well as development of teaching expertise over time. There were additional data that did not refer directly to the topic of teaching so much as to how indicators within the Teacher Quality Construct relate to each other. We discuss this data briefly to demonstrate empirically how individual indicators are interrelated by teachers to other indicators within and across components and are deemed by them to be significant contributors to the perceived qualities required of an early career teacher. The data demonstrating the interrelationship of the indicators echoes the statistical modelling presented in Chapter 5 and brings it to life through the voices of teachers. It provides qualitative insight to the quantitative data.

When collapsing open codes into axial codes patterns emerged where participants occasionally responded to the indicators by considering how they interacted with, supported, or enhanced other qualities that had been deemed more essential for ECTs. This perception, which took into account the component within which the removed indicators belonged, wasn't consistent across all responses. That is, there was no single secondary quality to which all removed indicators were related. We have chosen to discuss two as they provide insight to how respondents were interpreting the indicators as part of the overall construct.

Some respondents saw self-confidence as necessary for ECTs to build their resilience as teachers. Resilience refers to a teacher's strength and elasticity in working through difficulties and challenges, and self-confidence will contribute to a teacher's belief in their capacity to handle those challenges (Ahmad & Kutty, 2023). Conversely, resilience can also foster aspects of the 'self', including self-confidence (Gratacós et al., 2023; Neumann & Tillott, 2022). At the beginning of a teacher's career, "there will be a lot of knocks to their confidence due to interactions with students, parents and other staff members" (T106), and ECTs "need to be strong enough in that [these interactions] don't derail their self-beliefs about themselves" (T64). As T6 said, "it takes a lot to go into a classroom everyday and tackle the challenges of teaching", so without a modicum of self-confidence, "how will early career teachers bounce back after unsuccessful lessons and believe in what they are doing in their class-rooms" (T15)?

In other commentary, respondents explored how creativity relates to other qualities such as curiosity, cognition, and adaptability. Creativity can be understood to be inventiveness and innovation in how teachers approach or conceive of their teaching, and the other qualities related to creativity represent what motivates that creativity (curiosity), the thought processes involved in creative teaching approaches (cognition), and how that creativity influences a teacher's capacity to be flexible (adaptability). These opinions align strongly with research that attests to the need for teachers to cultivate creativity as "a form of personhood" (Tebaldi, 2024). Several respondents commented about how creativity is useful for ECTs as they adjust their teaching practice to suit their students' needs. Respondents considered creativity essential for "creating engaging learn-ing activities for students" (T30), "going with the flow in the classroom" (T105), to "think of a different way to approach a particular concept to ensure you can meet the needs of a range of student ability" (T47). It could also allow for "diversity of thought" (T21), "working around prob-lematic behaviours" (T60), and to "think divergently" (T26) as they explore their capacity in the classroom. These responses show how crea-tivity relates to the intellectual work of teaching (Rowe & Skourdoumbis, 2019), which takes us back to the opening proposition that teaching is complex and shows how the Teacher Quality Construct could reframe how teachers' work might be conceptualised.

## Conclusion

The data discussed in this chapter is limited by the small number of par-ticipant responses utilised for analysis, and as such it is not possible to come to any definite conclusions about how teacher qualities contribute to classroom readiness. However, the divergent views illustrate the lack of agreement in the profession about how classroom readiness is defined and echo the research representing classroom readiness as both a benchmark of mastery and a milestone at entry to the profession. The teachers' voices have clearly illustrated the difference between a view of the ECT stage as a step on a continuous trajectory of professional identity formation and skill development or the view of ECTs as merely qualified to be ready to teach. These dissonant opinions represent members of the teaching community with whom ECTs interact and through whom they are inducted into teaching. Though the data were collected in Australia, we suggest that similar patterns would emerge should the survey have been run with international participants.

The data raises challenges for ECTs and for the status of the profession. Shulman states that "the professional holds knowledge, not only of the capacity for skilled performance but of what and why. The teacher is not only a master of procedure but also of content and rationale, and capable of explaining why something is done" (1986, p. 13). If we agree with this, to be classroom ready is to be prepared for the work of a teacher, but it is also context dependent, ongoing, and managed within interactions of their teaching context. This ongoing negotiation of what it means to be classroom ready needs to be activated to support collegially-formed professional identities for teachers to thrive as adaptive, deliberative, agentive professionals (Lytle in Kosnik et al., 2013). As teachers change and improve, rather than relying on their own individual experiences to provide them with appropriate training and development, educational communities of practice and institutions could set such processes in place (Admiraal & Kittelsen Røberg, 2023).

Our data also confirms that the participating teachers have differing assumptions about how teacher quality is developed and nurtured. This finding raises a challenge to education systems in general as, if certain indicators of quality are presumed to develop with time and experience, all ECTs should have the same opportunities to have these qualities supported in their local contexts. However, while mentoring is seen as key to ECTs growth and survival (Beijaard & Meijer, 2017), not all ECTs are given the systematic opportunities they need to develop their emerging identities as teachers as they negotiate divergent conceptions of classroom readiness. The chapter has explored not only the ways in which the data reveals expectations of ECTs but also how these expectations have consequences for the formation of their future teacher identity. It also highlights the complex views teachers hold about teacher quality and the importance of clear and open discussion about these qualities for teachers at all career stages and contexts, but especially for those navigating the beginnings of their career. If adopted by systems, the Teacher Quality Construct could inform professional learning in ways that would support ECTs to grow into their roles as teachers as part of a community of practice as well as enhance the status of the profession.

## Key References

Alexander, C. (2018). Conceptions of readiness in initial teacher education: Quality, impact, standards and evidence in policy directives. In C. Wyatt-Smith & L. Adie (Eds.), *Innovation and accountability in teacher education* (pp. 97–113). Springer Nature. https://doi.org/10.1007/978-981-13-2026-2_7

Ludecke, M., & Cooper, R. (2023). Ready, or not? Graduate teachers' perceptions of their classroom readiness through a capstone assessment task. *Asia-Pacific Journal of Teacher Education*, *51*(2), 183–197. https://doi.org/10.1080/1359866X.2023.2177138

Mayer, D., Goodwin, A. L., & Mockler, N. (2021). Teacher education policy: Future research, teaching in contexts of super-diversity and early career teaching. In D. Mayer (Ed.), *Teacher education policy and research* (pp. 209–223). Springer Nature. https://doi.org/10.1007/978-981-16-3775-9_15

Shulman, L.S. (1986). Those who understand: Knowledge growth in teaching. *Educational Researcher*, *15*(2), 4–14.

Williams, M., & Moser, T. (2019). The art of coding and thematic exploration in qualitative research. *International Management Review*, *15*(1), 45–55.

# 7 Building a measurement scale for teacher quality to assess the predictive validity of teaching performance assessments

*Jim Tognolini and Janet Clinton*

## Introduction

While predictive validity is often considered the gold standard for measurement instruments, opportunities to measure it in relation to teacher quality have been elusive. The What's the Evidence (WtE) study offers an innovative approach to this challenge by establishing a foundational validation framework. This framework posits that when two robust measures of teacher quality - one a teaching performance assessment (TPA) (the Assessment for Graduate Teaching, or A*f*GT) and another a scale based on the Teacher Quality Construct - demonstrate significant correlation, they establish a compelling case for predictive validity. This relationship is particularly meaningful given that both measures of teacher quality are designed to be used at different points in the professional trajectory yet maintain theoretical and empirical connections.

The foundation of this framework rests on several interconnected elements. First, both measures incorporate research evidence and stakeholder perspectives, ensuring comprehensive construct validity. This integration creates a unified set of indicators that reflect both theoretical understanding and practical expertise. The validation process for each scale has demanded consensus among stakeholders and careful analysis of indicator relationships, all achieved through rigorous standard-setting and benchmarking procedures.

The relationship between the A*f*GT and the Teacher Quality Construct (TQC) is particularly powerful because both measures share critical characteristics. They incorporate research-based evidence and stakeholder input, utilise sound psychometric principles, and employ similar comparative methodologies. The sequential nature of these assessments, combined with their shared theoretical foundations, allows for meaningful interpretation of results based on their temporal relationships. Hence exploring the correlation between the A*f*GT and TQC indicators presents a unique opportunity to establish both concurrent and predictive validity.

DOI: 10.4324/9781003542575-7

When these instruments are administered contemporaneously, they provide concurrent validity (Lin & Yao, 2024) through correlation coefficients. More significantly, their temporal relationship - with A*f*GT measuring future teaching quality and WtE assessing experienced teacher quality - creates a logical sequence that supports steps to predictive validity claims. The chapter explores the logic behind the process of constructing measurement rubrics and a scale of teacher quality during the WtE study and then presents a series of propositions to consider the place of predictive validity and the future development of a validation framework for teacher quality.

## Constructing measurement rubrics

Measurement rubrics help to differentiate growth at each level graduation in a construct via a set of pre-defined performance level descriptors (Egan et al., 2012; Greatorex, 2003). In this way they operationalise what it means to grow or progress and therefore can be a reference for locating the amount of the construct present relative to the performance level descriptor. Measurement rubrics are valuable for understanding the construct that is being measured and documenting growth toward attainment of 'more' of the construct being measured, rather than just providing a score in isolation (Bennett, 2019; Brookhart & Chen, 2015; Herman & Linn, 2014; Messick, 1975).

In this book, measurement rubrics refer to a designed framework (with a limited number of descriptive performance levels) to show what growth in teacher quality will look like along a continuum of performance that describes growth in the construct of teacher quality. Describing a clear interpretation of what growth looks like along a continuum (as represented by a measurement rubric) is challenging. It requires numerous iterations to arrive at a consistent description of growth for the construct being measured (Bennett et al., 2012; Tognolini & Davidson, 2013; Tognolini & Stanley, 2007).

Defining a clear description of the construct should be grounded in modern measurement theory (Andrich & Marais, 2019; Bond & Fox, 2007; Bond et al., 2020). Tognolini (2018) argued that a definition should include the appropriate knowledge, skills, or understanding of the content or generic skills that can be observed. These are the direct components (and indicators) that will constitute the measurement rubric. Such components and indicators then provide "a distinguishing property or characteristic..., by which its quality can be judged or estimated, or by which a decision or classification may be made" (Sadler, 1987, p. 194).

The following steps outline the basic processes for designing and developing a measurement rubric.

**Step 1:** Define the construct that you want to measure.

**Step 2:** Decide on the components and indicators that represent the construct. These components and indicators provide the basis for generating the evidence for the performance specified in the definition.

**Step 3:** Develop descriptions of performance for each performance level of the construct. This could also involve, in some cases, describing the performance level of each component and even each indicator, if the intention of the measurement rubric is to provide explicit feedback on each component and indicator.

Step 4: Build the evidential argument for validating the rubric as a legitimate measure.

These steps relate to building the measurement scale that underpins the measurement rubric. We have not discussed assessment of teachers at this stage. This is consistent with measurement in the physical sciences where first the measurement scale (such as a ruler, or thermometer) is built and then the measurement is carried out. Assessment is an inclusive term, which refers to all those processes used to collect data, build evidence, and make judgments about teacher performance on indicators that comprise the construct (Tognolini & Davidson, 2013; Tognolini & Stanley, 2007). It is stressed that the steps in constructing and validating measurement rubrics described here can be used in any measurement system to build measures for any construct that is valued.

### Modern measurement theory, measurement scales and rubrics

Modern measurement theory provides a framework for understanding and measuring constructs (also called latent variables) through the use of tests and other assessments that provide observable responses that are theoretically related to the underlying construct of interest; in our case, teacher quality. Rasch theory is one of multiple theories of measurement (Andrich and Marais, 2019). The measurement rubric developed and used for measuring teacher quality in this book is based on modern measurement theory as operationalised through Rasch theory (Andrich & Marais, 2019; Bond & Fox, 2007; Bond et al., 2020). The Rasch model is a mathematical representation of Rasch Theory.

There are several features which accrue to measuring in the social sciences where the measurement scale has been constructed in accord with the Rasch model. The most important feature is referred to as specific objectivity (Rasch, 1960). If the data obtained from the teachers completing the measures of each of the indicators conform to the Rasch Model, then the measure of the teachers on the construct is independent of the measures used. Specific objectivity is unique to the class of Rasch models.

This is because each of the indicator measures in our study relate to the same construct; so, they are on the same scale. What this means in practice is that you can use different combinations of indicators of teacher quality and the overall result will be referenced to the TQC scale. A measurement scale is a linear continuum partitioned into equal units which provide the measurements, and the scaling locates the teachers on the scale (Andrich & Marais, 2019).

### Constructing the measurement scale for teacher quality

In the case of the WtE study we have defined a construct of teacher quality (Step 1). It refers to a composite of characteristics and attributes, knowledges and intelligences possessed and practiced reflexively by an individual. Chapters 1 and 3 described our initial definition of teacher quality and the process we used to ensure our construct was evidence informed.

We have also described the 37 indicators that represent and align with the Intellectual, Interpersonal, Affective, and Intrapersonal construct components (Step 2). Chapters 4 and 5 demonstrated the identification and rationale for nominating the 30 indicators as most essential for early career teachers (ECTs). It is worth noting that the generalisability of this measurement rubric is limited to the context in which it was developed (in this case, the New South Wales education system). However, the process described is generalisable to all contexts and all constructs.

In order to enact Step 3, to develop descriptions of performance for each performance level of the TQC, the WtE project trialled two distinct processes. In 2023, the first process aimed to collect data from paired participants who gave informed ethical consent. The pairs were ECTs matched to the principals from the schools in which they were employed. Principals' on balance judgment appraisals of ECTs as outstanding, above average, average and below average were collected on a simple survey. The team hoped to collect from the principals descriptions of the characteristics that led to their appraisals which could be used to build a rich 'image' of teacher quality across the nominated performance levels. The intention was to build a regression model to assign regression weights to the indicator measures. This sequence of actions is a well-recognised process for building performance levels (standards) in a traditional standard setting process (Angoff, 1971; Cizek, 2012). Unfortunately, the participation rate was too low and there were insufficient data to generate meaningful conclusions. So, this attempt at building the measurement scale was abandoned and a new process was devised using new participant recruitment and sampling techniques.

The second process of devising descriptors of performance levels was conducted in 2024. Fifty one participants (41 teachers and 10 school leaders) were recruited and took part in focus group/workshops to establish benchmarking standards across four levels. This phase utilised a subset of the original TQC measurement instrument with the common component being 14 items from the measure of Reflective practice. Three groups of participants acting as judges were asked to build a mental image of characteristics of teachers on the borderline between one of three pairs of performance levels: e.g. Outstanding and Above Average, Above Average and Average, and Average and Below Average (Figure 7.1).

Each 'judge' then independently recorded the responses they thought their imagined teachers would choose for 14 Likert statements. Next, the judges for each borderline were brought together to share the reasoning behind their cut-scores. Discrepancies were discussed in terms of the image of the borderline teacher that the judge had in their mind and its relationship to the level of response they thought appropriate to make explicit the construct of Reflective practice. Judges could either retain their original estimates or change them to reflect changed understanding of the question under consideration (Figure 7.2).

The final cut-score for each level of performance (or the borderline) was determined by calculating the average of the scores proposed by all judges at the end of the standard setting workshops.

Figure 7.3 shows the distribution of the judges estimates for all 3 borderline cut-scores. There were 14 statements in the Reflective practice questionnaire and respondents were asked to rate each of the statements as follows: Almost always, Frequently, Occasionally, and Almost never which were then rated as 3, 2, 1 and 0 respectively. This means that there was a possible total score of 42 across the 14 items. It can be seen from Figure 7.3 that the estimates of the judges who scored teachers on the border between Above average and Outstanding (n=15 judges) were 36, 34, 33, 29, 29, 28, 28, 27, 26, 25, 25, 23, 23, 21, 20. The average of these estimates was 27.1, so a score at 28 or above would be considered to be indicative of teachers of Outstanding quality. Similarly, Figure 7.3 shows that a score of 21 up to and including 27 would be indicative of Above average teacher quality, a score of 10 up to and including 20 would be indicative of Average teacher quality, and a score of 0 up to and including 9 would be indicative of Below average teacher quality.

It must be stressed that this process is intended to be a gathering of evidence to support feasibility of the methods. There were only a limited number of judges, a reduced measure of only one indicator (Reflective practice) and limited time for the judges to socialise the process of standard setting and come to closer convergence of the cut-score. The outcome demonstrates early steps in building the measurement scale. At this stage with only one small set of data it is not possible to conceptualise measurement of the construct fully because the 'images' (descriptors) that capture the performance levels are far too underdeveloped. However, as the process of collecting more data continues, and additional measures are

Step 1

We are creating a new measure of teacher quality. We need your help to create a common understanding of the concept. Please think of an image of a teacher who is right on the border of the two scale points of teacher quality. Eg. Above Average/Average. Without discussing this with anyone else, note down some key words and phrases to help you capture that image

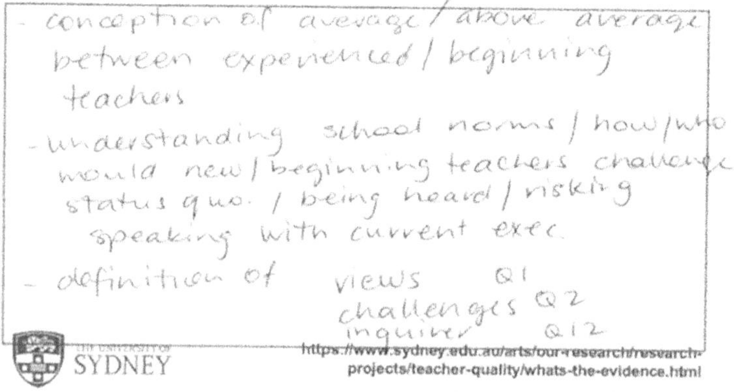


Discussion

How did the group results differ from your original concept words of the borderline teacher?





https://www.sydney.edu.au/arts/our-research/research-projects/teacher-quality/whats-the-evidence.html

*Figure 7.1* Notes from image creation exercise for above average/average borderline

Step 2. Imagine you are the borderline teacher. How would you respond to the questions below?

| A Critically Reflective Teacher: | Almost Always | Frequently | Occasionally | Almost Never |
| --- | --- | --- | --- | --- |
| SQ: Engages in constructive criticism of their teaching | | X | | |
| 1. Challenges status quo norms and practices, especially with respect to power and control | | | X | |
| 2. Views practice within the broader sociological, cultural, historical, and political contexts | X → | X | | |
| 3. Addresses issues of equity and social justice that arise in and outside of the classroom. | | X | | |
| 4. Considers the ethical ramifications of classroom policies and practices. | | X | | |
| 5. Acknowledges the social and political consequences of one's teaching. | | | X | |
| 6. Acknowledges that teaching practices and policies can either contribute to, or hinder, the realisation of a more just and humane society. | | X → | X | |
| 7. Observes self in the process of thinking. *reflective* | | | X | |
| 8. Is aware of incongruence between beliefs and actions and takes action to rectify. | | X | | |
| 9. Challenges assumptions about students and expectations for students. | | X | | |
| 10. Encourages socially responsible actions in their students. | X | | | |
| 11. Recognises assumptions and premises underlying beliefs. | | X | | |
| 12. Is an active inquirer, both critiquing current conclusions and generating new hypotheses. | | X | | |
| 13. Calls commonly-held beliefs into question. | | | X | |
| 14. Suspends judgments to consider all options. | | | X | |

*Figure 7.2* Scoring sheet for the 14 item questionnaire showing changed rating after discussion

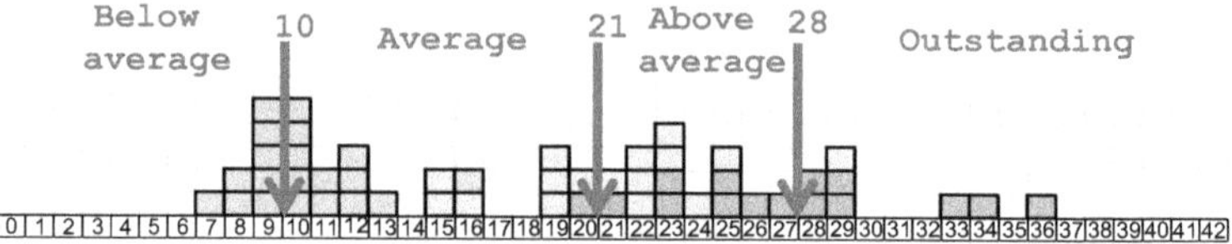


*Figure 7.3* Judges' estimates of teacher quality cut scores

explored, the performance levels will be more richly developed and become capable of showing what growth teacher quality looks like. The process makes growth in the construct more transparent and accessible.

The second source of data collected in this process was the results from 42 end of degree pre-service teachers (PSTs) from two Sydney-based universities who completed self-assessments using the same 14-item instrument on Reflective practice that was used in the standard setting exercise. The third source of data were the AfGT results for these PSTs that were collected to assist in testing a process to assess predictive validity.

Step 4 required us to build evidential arguments for validating the measurement rubric as a legitimate measure. The preliminary stage of building the evidential argument is covered in Chapters 4 and 5 of this book. In Chapter 5 we provided evidence that the indicators that had been identified in the Delphi process were related to the construct of teacher quality. This, along with the various focus group discussions of the relationship between the indicators and teacher quality illustrated in Chapter 4 provide a basis for the development of the validation argument for teacher quality. The validation process will continue as more evidence is generated over time to support the argument that the measurement rubric is measuring the construct it is intended to measure.

Messick (1989) described validity as an "integrated evaluative judgment of the degree to which empirical evidence and theoretical rationales support the adequacy and appropriateness of inferences and actions based on test scores or other modes of assessment" (p. 13). Validating a measurement rubric involves using both theoretical and empirical approaches in an integrated multi-step process to collecting the evidence to support the argument that the scale is really measuring the construct that it is designed to measure. The earlier chapters in this book provide a chronicle of evidence that supports the validity of the teacher quality measurement rubric. Thus far we have demonstrated the integrated processes that can be used to conceptualise a construct, identify its components and indicators and define appropriate performance level criteria that describe the construct or components, or even individual indicators. All of the stakeholders and participant groups have contributed in different ways to the processes of producing a measurement rubric of teacher quality. The resulting current draft of the rubric provides some theoretical evidence regarding the content validity of the rubric itself as the arguments that have led to version changes have focused upon making sure that the rubric is fit for purpose and is measuring what to is supposed to be measuring.

In the following section we describe the empirical evidential argument basis of the validation process for our measurement rubric for teacher quality. The measures of the indicators that are used locate the teachers on the teacher quality scale (e.g., the questionnaires or other instruments used to assess performance on the various indicators) must also have validity evidence to support the argument that they are measuring the indicator that they purport to measure.

If the measurement rubric for teacher quality has an evidential argument that satisfies most, or all of the requirements of reliability and validity described in this brief description, then there can be a strong degree of assurance that the measurement rubric for teacher quality is accurate and fit for purpose.

## Converting the measurement rubric to a measurement scale

We applied a Rasch Model to data derived from the administration of the modified questionnaire (14 statements) for the indicator of Reflective practice to 79 final year Master of Teaching students to determine difficulties of these statements and use these difficulties to operationally define the measurement scale. The model also generated a location (measure of teacher quality) on the same scale. One of the features of the Rasch Model is that it locates teachers and statements on the same scale so that they can be directly compared.

Figure 7.4 shows the teacher quality scale produced by the Rasch Model.

The scale in Figure 7.4 features two grouped distributions: one for the 14 statements (shown as 42 score points), arranged along the bottom of the scale's central horizontal line) and one on the top for the 79 teachers who completed the questionnaire. The statements to the left of the measurement scale are those that teachers found easy to agree with; in other words, these are the aspects of Reflective practice teachers are likely to display in their classrooms as a matter of routine. For example, the statement that most teachers found easy to agree with was "I am a teacher who: Encourages socially responsible actions in their students" (Statement 10). Movement to right on the measurement scale would be represented by those aspects of Reflective practice which are least likely to be embedded in a teacher's practices or alternatively more likely to be part of an effective teacher's arsenal. For example, "I am a teacher who: Challenges status quo

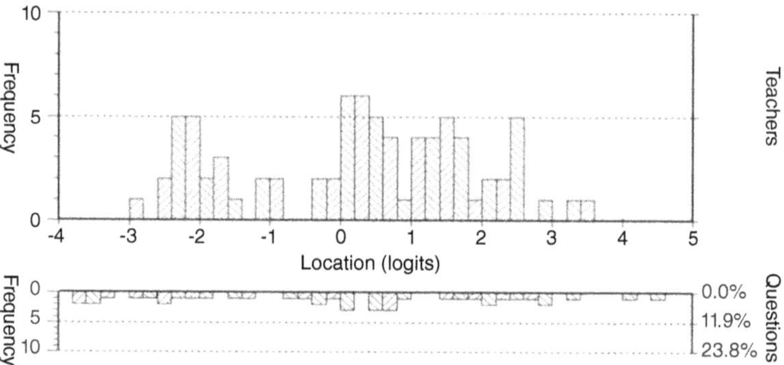


*Figure 7.4* Teacher-statement distribution across the teacher quality scale as reflected by the Reflective practice measure

norms and practices, especially with respect to power and control" (Statement 1).

Figure 7.4 also shows that teachers who scored highly (i.e., those with the most aspects of Reflective practice embedded in their usual classroom activities as reflected in their responses) are located to the right on the distribution of teachers, while those with fewer aspects of Reflective practice in their classroom appear to the left of the (top) distribution. In Chapter 3 research evidence supports Reflective practice as an indicator of teacher quality. In Chapter 5, we showed a relationship between Reflective practice and teacher quality. Now the Rasch Model has been used to produce a measurement scale for teacher quality whereby responses to an indicator of teacher quality can be used to locate teachers directly on the scale.

Table 7.1 shows the statements of Reflective practice in the order of those statements that were easiest for teachers to agree with to those that were most challenging i.e., those where teachers with the most quality would be likely to agree.

A feature of the Rasch Model is that the raw score, obtained by adding the responses of the teachers to each of the questions is a sufficient statistic for generating the location (in logits) of the teacher on the measurement scale. A logit is the unit used to calibrate the scale. The scale is an equal interval measurement scale and can be thought of as a measurement scale with the properties of a measure in the physical sciences.

The Rasch Model produces a table that converts raw scores to scale score (logits) on the measurement scale. Table 7.2 provides the raw score to scale score table that was produced as part of the analysis of the current data.

*Table 7.1* Reflective practice questions and average locations on the teacher quality scale

| Statement number | Statement | Average scale value (logits) |
|---|---|---|
| CR10 | I am a teacher who: Encourages socially responsible actions in their students. | −1.65 |
| CR9 | I am a teacher who: Challenges assumptions about students and expectations for students. | −0.59 |
| CR7 | I am a teacher who: Observes self in the process of thinking. | −0.52 |
| CR4 | I am a teacher who: Considers the ethical ramifications of classroom policies and practices. | −0.35 |
| CR3 | I am a teacher who: Addresses issues of equity and social justice that arise in and outside of the classroom. | −0.24 |
| CR5 | I am a teacher who: Acknowledges the social and political consequences of one's teaching. | −0.22 |
| CR6 | I am a teacher who: Acknowledges that teaching practices and policies can either contribute to, or hinder, the realisation of a more just and humane society. | −0.22 |
| CR14 | I am a teacher who: Suspends judgments to consider all options. | −0.1 |
| CR2 | I am a teacher who: Views practice within the broader sociological, cultural, historical, and political contexts. | 0 |
| CR11 | I am a teacher who: Recognises assumptions and premises underlying beliefs. | 0.02 |
| CR8 | I am a teacher who: Is aware of incongruence between beliefs and actions and takes action to rectify. | 0.48 |
| CR12 | I am a teacher who: Addresses issues of equity and social justice that arise in and outside of the classroom. | 0.75 |
| CR13 | I am a teacher who: Calls commonly held beliefs into question. | 1.09 |
| CR1 | I am a teacher who: Challenges status quo norms and practices, especially with respect to power and control. | 1.56 |

The borderline raw scores obtained from the standard setting exercise were: 28, 21 and 10. These correspond to scale values on the teacher quality measurement scale of 1.261, 0.070 and −2.089 respectively.

Figure 7.5 shows these borderline scores located on the TQC measurement scale.

This analysis is designed to demonstrate a proof of concept rather than suggest that the distribution reflects any generalisable distribution of teacher quality across a specified population of teachers. The teachers who sat the single indicator of teacher quality (Reflective practice measure) were

*Table 7.2* Raw score on Reflective practice questionnaire to scale score on teacher quality scale

| Raw score | Scale value (logits) | Raw score | Scale value(logits) | Raw score | Scale value(logits) |
|---|---|---|---|---|---|
| 0 | −5.931 | 15 | −1.026 | 30 | 1.625 |
| 1 | −5.086 | 16 | −0.831 | 31 | 1.817 |
| 2 | −4.476 | 17 | −0.642 | 32 | 2.017 |
| 3 | −4.034 | 18 | −0.458 | 33 | 2.228 |
| 4 | −3.673 | 19 | −0.278 | 34 | 2.452 |
| 5 | −3.359 | 20 | −0.103 | 35 | 2.693 |
| 6 | −3.075 | 21 | 0.070 | 36 | 2.955 |
| 7 | −2.810 | 22 | 0.240 | 37 | 3.247 |
| 8 | −2.560 | 23 | 0.409 | 38 | 3.579 |
| 9 | −2.320 | 24 | 0.577 | 39 | 3.970 |
| 10 | −2.089 | 25 | 0.745 | 40 | 4.458 |
| 11 | −1.864 | 26 | 0.915 | 41 | 5.133 |
| 12 | −1.646 | 27 | 1.086 | 42 | 6.066 |
| 13 | −1.434 | 28 | 1.261 | | |
| 14 | −1.227 | 29 | 1.440 | | |

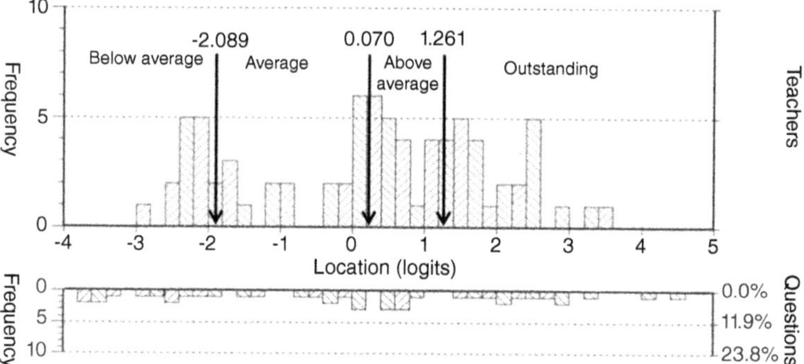


*Figure 7.5* Distribution of teacher quality as reflected by the Reflective practice measure attempted by 79 teachers

Masters of Teaching students at end of their degree and not early career teachers or experienced teachers and we only used a sample of the statements that comprised the Reflective practice questionnaire. The next section shows how we intend to equate the measures of the other indicators using the Rasch Model.

## Rasch theory and equating

The development of Rasch models arose from an equating problem related to the need to compare reading tests, administered to the same pupils at different grades, to measure the improvement in reading ability (Rasch, 1960). When items in different tests have been shown to measure the same property and shown to fit the requirements of the Rasch model, then they can be transformed onto a single measurement scale. In our case, we identified 30 indicators and showed that they measure a common construct of teacher quality. These indicators are equivalent to the different tests in Rasch's original problem.

Once the indicators are on a common measurement scale, the scores that result from any of the measures are automatically equated and no further collection or analysis of data is needed. Just like with the traditional methods of test equating, Rasch theory equating uses common items or students to place the different tests or indicators onto the common scale.

Figure 7.6 shows the schematic representation of the common measure design we will use to transform each of the indicators onto the teacher quality measurement scale.

Figure 7.6 shows a matrix which has 3 of the 30 measures of indicators across the top: measure of cognition, measure of adaptability, measure of reflective practice. On completion this will show all the various measures for the 30 indicators in our study. The vertical axis shows teachers stratified into samples of 300. The first strata of teachers would complete measures (questionnaires) related to cognition and adaptability. The second strata would complete measures of adaptability and reflective practice. The common measure, in this case adaptability, enables all 3 measures to be located on a common teacher quality measurement scale. This process can be replicated using different strata of teachers to locate all the measures on the teacher quality scale.

Figure 7.7 shows conceptually how the TQC might be represented.

More extensive processes to strengthen the content validation of the rubric are needed such as additional focus groups comprising a wide range of stakeholders to continue to refine the scale. The process outcomes from these focus groups will inform the researchers responsible for building upon the current measurement rubric. It is important to evaluate the comments and suggestions regarding the rubric's structure, documenting all arguments that either support changes or explain why certain changes were not incorporated into the measurement rubric. Other evidence will emerge from interactions with teams and schools in different contexts as they evaluate the suitability of the measurement rubric for various settings. It is important that this evidence be collected systematically and incorporated into the evidential argument that underpins the case for the rubrics' validity.

Subsequently different type of validity evidence will emerge once the measurement scale has been developed and is ready for use by teachers

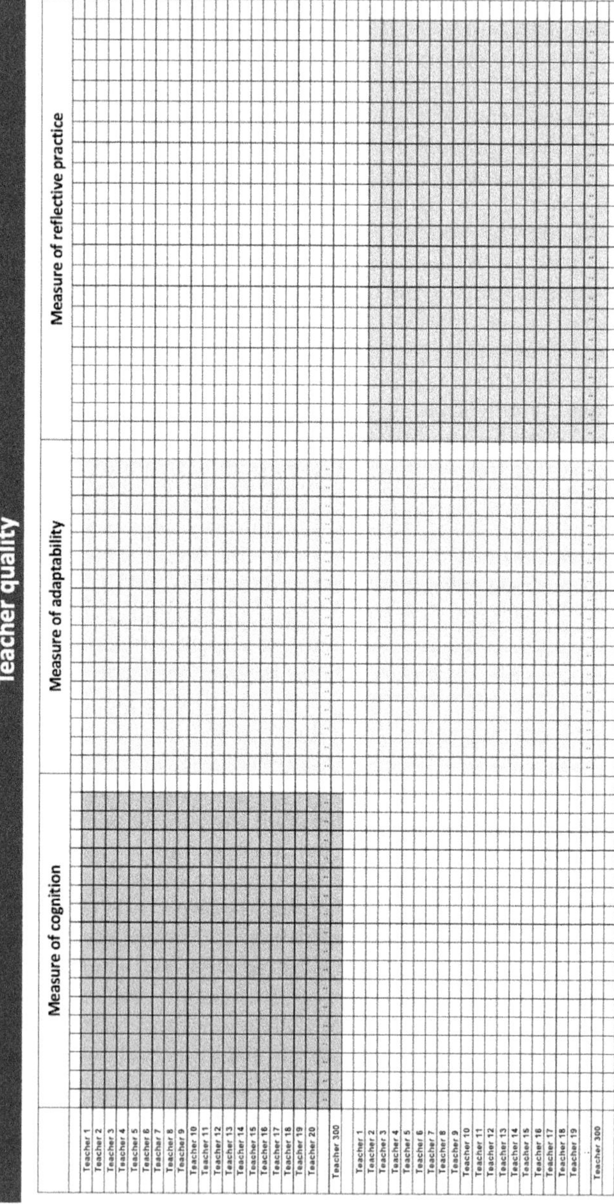


*Figure 7.6* Common measure equating design

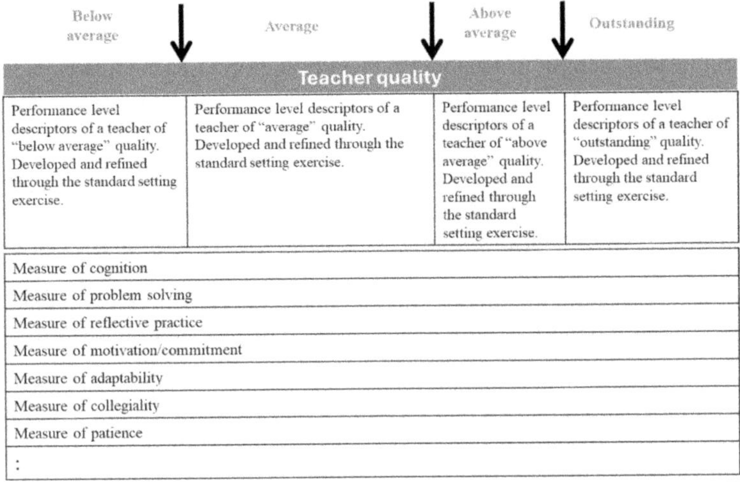



| Performance level descriptors of a teacher of "below average" quality. Developed and refined through the standard setting exercise. | Performance level descriptors of a teacher of "average" quality. Developed and refined through the standard setting exercise. | Performance level descriptors of a teacher of "above average" quality. Developed and refined through the standard setting exercise. | Performance level descriptors of a teacher of "outstanding" quality. Developed and refined through the standard setting exercise. |
| --- | --- | --- | --- |
| Measure of cognition | | | |
| Measure of problem solving | | | |
| Measure of reflective practice | | | |
| Measure of motivation/commitment | | | |
| Measure of adaptability | | | |
| Measure of collegiality | | | |
| Measure of patience | | | |
| ⋮ | | | |

*Figure 7.7* Conceptual representation of the teacher quality scale

and schools in the assessment and measurement process. Schools will then be able to choose indicators that align with their philosophy, context, and stage of development. All schools would not have to have the same measures. The results could be analysed and discussed at the level of the individual indicator so that the discussion focused only on the indicators that have been selected by the specific school. However, the deidentified measure of teacher quality could be collected at a system, state, or national level as an evolving distribution of teacher quality. Consequently, the continual strengthening of this measurement scale beyond would support systematic collection of evidence of teacher quality for the first time in any system and potentially anywhere in the world.

In the next section an Australian TPA, the AfGT, is used as an illustrative context in which, with an independent measure of teacher quality, it would become possible to augment the validation frameworks of measures of teaching effectiveness beyond the traditional validation measures of content and construct validity to include predictive validity.

### Designing processes to establish predictive validity for the AfGT

Predictive validity is defined as the evidence indicating how accurately test data collected at one time can predict criterion measures that are obtained on a different occasion (American Educational Research Association et al., 2014). Analysis of predictive validity involves calculating correlation coefficients between the initial assessment scores and the subsequent outcome measures, while controlling for relevant variables through modelling. Determining the predictive validity of a TPA requires the systematic collection and analysis of data that demonstrates the assessment's ability to predict teaching effectiveness in relation to teacher quality. A standard setting exercise that involves members from the sector is a critical element to ensure the benchmarks represent the on-balance judgement of all stakeholders. Gathering multiple forms of data from a range of stakeholders over time is key. These various data points serve as the criterion measures against which the predictive power of the assessment can be evaluated.

The A*f*GT is a TPA developed and implemented by a consortium of institutions led by the University of Melbourne. It was founded on several key principles that reflect best practices in teacher education assessment. The development was guided by a commitment to authentic assessment that genuinely reflects the complexities of classroom teaching. The A*f*GT was able to be designed through strengthened collegial relationships with colleagues in different parts of the country, in institutions with different program types, delivery models and histories (McGraw et al., 2021). Central to its design was the principle of evidence-based practice, ensuring that pre-service teachers can demonstrate their ability to collect, analyse, and use evidence of student learning to inform their teaching decisions. The assessment was strategically structured around the Australian Professional Standards for Teachers (APST) and underwent rigorous validation processes to ensure its alignment, reliability and effectiveness. The development process included multiple pilot studies and refinements based on feedback from various stakeholders, including mentor teachers, teacher educators, and PSTs. At an instrument-level, the A*f*GT is robust and coherent, and at item-level, the A*f*GT demonstrates well-ordered statistical parameters with strong and reliable test information. The A*f*GT has a systematic approach to continuous review of the instrument's reliability and validity.

The A*f*GT has gained recognition for its robust design and alignment with both theoretical frameworks and practical teaching requirements, leading to its adoption by 15 institutions across Australia and its endorsement by the Australian Institute for Teaching and School Leadership (AITSL). In addition, based on consortium-wide feedback, the A*f*GT has been accepted as a valid, reliable and fair teaching performance assessment instrument. The consortium has demonstrated that the process of completing the TPA influences pre-service teachers' reflection and professional reasoning, and expands their knowledge of how their teaching improves their students' learning (Kriewaldt et al., 2021), however, up to this point, there has been no evidence to support the implied relationship between the A*f*GT and early career teacher performance. While it can be argued that TPAs nationally and internationally have impacted positively on the profession, relating such measures to teacher quality is still elusive.

It is acknowledged that the TPAs in the Australian case reflect broadly the content of some of the APSTs and that the TQC introduces other qualities that could be considered essential for ECTs. This raises the issue of what will be counted as acceptable evidence for how teacher quality will be measured in the future.

## Conclusion and propositions for future research

The WtE study has presented not only a rubric and scale of teacher quality built on a rigorous process supported by modern measurement theory but also a proof of concept approach to generate predictive validity for a TPA. The initial testing has advanced an approach to predictive validity that simultaneously employs two robust measures of teacher quality. By creating a strong measure with established construct validity and comparing it against another validated measure of teacher quality, we argued the overall validity framework could be strengthened. This approach primarily establishes concurrent validity - a form of criterion-related validity that evaluates how well a new measurement tool correlates with an established measure when administered contemporaneously (Lin & Yao, 2024).

The idea was tested by examining the relationship between the AfGT and the TQC. This relationship is particularly significant because the AfGT measures preservice teachers' readiness to teach, while the TQC focuses on experienced teacher quality. The process created an opportunity to calculate correlation coefficients between the two measures. We demonstrated that a predictor of teacher quality and a related measure could be used to create an opportunity to calculate correlation coefficient and thus generated an argument for a proxy measure of predictive validity. However, as the recruitment sample size in the final stage of the WtE study was small, it was not possible calculate a reliable correlation coefficient. Despite this, we argue that the WtE study has created a foundational validation framework for teacher quality that will continue to be refined, is feasible, and could be easily scalable. Now, we suggest the need to expand the validation framework for measures of teacher quality in the future.

Our argument is simple. Any measure of teacher quality needs to have its foundation in an evidence-informed framework that is seen as valid and acceptable to all members across various contexts. It will be important to predict, monitor and address as quickly as possible any unintended consequences of measurement processes that would decrease the value of the measures and the validity of the measurement rubric. As existing measures are validated and new measures of indicators that do not currently exist are developed, they will provide further evidence that could challenge the existing measurement rubric. This continuous process of building, refining and validating the new measures and the interaction of those data with the measurement rubric should be used to monitor the quality of the measurement rubrics and maximise the validity of the measures.

Therefore, in the future we propose the creation of a strong validation process building on the outcomes of the WtE study, which is critical for the complex world of teacher quality. The advantages of a refined validation framework for teacher quality would be:

- Provision of a systematic approach to evaluating measurement tools
- Establishment of clear standards for quality assessment
- Identification of potential weaknesses or gaps in standards and assessments
- Systematic documentation of validation process
- Replication and verification
- Strengthened research credibility

The WtE study has demonstrated a process for building a measurement rubric for teacher quality. The process could be adopted locally to support assessment of predictive validity, however, it could also be used more broadly by different systems for other purposes. The strength of the work is its research grounding in modern measurement theory, and its empirical evidence base, which has collected data from stakeholders in the profession. However, the work is not complete. We argue that the system of assessment and measurement of teacher quality could be developed to become more seamless from entry into an initial teacher education program through career development so that measures of teacher quality would be collected at different points in the temporal career trajectory. In addition, though establishing predictive validity is essential, we also suggest that a validation framework for identifying new measures of teacher quality is now critical.

## Key References

Andrich, D., & Marais, I. (2019). *A course in Rasch measurement theory: Measuring in the educational, social and health sciences.* Springer. https://doi.org/10.1007/978-981-13-7496-8

Cizek, G. J. (2012). *Setting performance standards: Foundations, methods, and innovations.* Routledge.

Kriewaldt, J., Walker, R., Morey, V., & Morrison, C. (2021). Activating and reinforcing graduates' capabilities: Early lessons learned from a teaching performance assessment. *The Australian Educational Researcher, 48,* 681–696. https://doi.org/10.1007/s13384-020-00418-4

Lin, W. L., & Yao, G. (2024). Concurrent validity. In *Encyclopedia of quality of life and well-being research* (pp. 1303–1304). Springer International Publishing.

Rasch, G. (1960). *Probabilistic models for some intelligence and attainment tests.* University of Chicago.

# 8 Shifting the discourse of teacher quality

*Rachel White, Louisa Peralta, and Christopher Day*

## Introduction

Previous chapters in this book have provided a comprehensive discussion of the What's the Evidence (WtE) study, a four-year project (2021-2024) funded by the NSW Department of Education and reported implications of its findings for new conceptualisations of teacher quality. The project connected with early career teachers (ECTs) through to school leaders and educational stakeholders from regulatory bodies and educational departments to provide insight and validation of the Teacher Quality Construct. The chapters focused on how the research utilised:

1 A scoping review to build and test a new construct of teacher quality (i.e., Teacher Quality Construct)
2 A modified Delphi process and Confirmatory Factor Analysis to validate the construct; and
3 The use of the evidence-informed construct to develop a process to test the predictive validity of an Australian Teaching Performance Assessment.

The study demonstrates the first attempted process of developing a validated research-informed Teacher Quality Construct, which was influenced by the voices of a range of stakeholders. It is clear from previous academic research that the concept of 'teacher quality' is a contested space. Yet, it is also clear from the committed involvement of varied cross sectoral groups over the length of the study, that this work is highly valued by the profession and is seen as critical to the future development of the sector. In a high stakes accountability context, it has addressed a gap in the field by taking on the challenge of defining and measuring teacher quality. As a whole, this book represents a theoretically informed and practice-oriented opportunity to speak to the negative discourse that inflects discussions of teacher quality. It avoids the limited emphasis that is often placed on teaching when talking about what teachers know and do. Instead, it views teaching

DOI: 10.4324/9781003542575-8

as "a humanistic endeavour" (Simpson et al., 2022, p. 2) and promotes a shared understanding of an innovative, holistic conceptualisation of teacher quality that offers greater insight to what being a teacher encompasses. This chapter will explore how the world-leading research findings can enable educators, from early career through to school leadership, to better navigate the tensions between teacher role, teacher identity, and teacher quality within the broad contexts of external mandates, such as professional teaching standards, school cultures, and their own understandings of teachers' professional role and identity.

## The standards agenda: Tensions and possibilities

There is consensus that economic rationalisation has contributed to "the rise of performance cultures which, are expressed through increased accountability, and the continued imposition of teacher standards" (Sachs, 2016, p. 414), creating, in some contexts, the sense of a "tick-box professionalism" (Goepel, 2012, p. 489). Recent school reform and changes in teacher education programs worldwide have been driven by globalisation and resultant social, scientific, technological and cultural challenges, which have increased governmental pressure to ensure students do well in national and international assessments by enhancing the quality of teachers and their teaching. Around the world, national policies have become a key motivator for the teaching profession to embrace standards as an important means of defining, regulating, and developing the skills and qualities of profession. Currently there are standards either being developed or in use in Australia, England, Scotland, New Zealand, United States of America, Canada, Singapore, China, Hong Kong, and Pakistan, among other countries. Nations and educative systems are increasingly creating monitoring structures and other regulatory mechanisms to ensure conformity and standardise teachers' practices (Adoniou & Gallagher, 2017; Goodwin, 2021; Sachs, 2013).

Professional standards and other means of defining, regulating, and monitoring professional knowledge and behaviour are now part of education systems around the world and demand skilful navigation by school leaders and teachers to overcome inevitable tensions that arise between "individual and social norms in educational contexts" (Glasswell & Ryan, 2017, pp. 24-25). Principals and other school executives are responsible for ensuring schools function effectively, within the confines of systemic policies and sociocultural expectations (Connolly et al., 2019). For example, educational leaders may 'comply' unquestioningly, or 'enact', or they may interpret and translate expectations into school cultures so that they question policies in order to become better informed and raise the status of the profession (Forde et al., 2016). Educational leaders may also exercise agency and influence (Torrance & Forde, 2017), acknowledging the gaps in a teacher's experience, context, and history that are unrecognised in teaching standards. It is in this process of 'enactment' of teaching standards, with the application of professional judgement and nuance, that the indicators of teacher quality could be used in the future by teachers, mentors, and school leaders to navigate the gaps between teacher role and identity in a reflective and discursive manner.

The development of professional teaching standards has been criticised by scholars who view them as "both as a way to improve the teaching profession and to control teachers' practice" (Hilton et al., 2013, p. 432); ensuring teacher quality as well as implementing compliance to externally mandated expectations (Appel, 2020; Ball, 2003; Fu & Clarke, 2019). These standards are critiqued as "underpinned by broad assumptions about effective practice" (Forde et al., 2016, p. 23) that may not be designed or used strictly for the purpose of developing the profession. They may, for example, over simplify measurement by implying that there is a formula for educational success (Call, 2020) by providing benchmarks for professionalism (Goodwin, 2021), which are overly prescriptive in stating what teachers should know and be able to do.

However, standards also have the capacity to be aspirational (Torrance & Forde, 2017) by providing descriptions and indicators of what knowledge and skills teachers need to develop to move into 'higher levels' of leadership and responsibilities. They can express a shared understanding and definition of teaching (Call, 2020), for the benefit of educators as well as establishing role expectations and definitions in the school and broader community and socio-cultural context. Where a common language of a profession is shared (Adoniou & Gallagher, 2017) it can also provide a career framework for educators, signposting how standards and competencies can be used to support productive professional development (Forde et al., 2016). Despite this positive view however, as critics have pointed out, rather than creating and utilising standards as a means of developing an aspirational workforce, their presence can make the profession lean further into a culture of regulation and surveillance (Sachs, 2013; Torrance & Forde, 2017), causing schools themselves to create internal monitoring systems which reflect those created externally. Together, these ensure that teachers' expectations of themselves as professionals become closely aligned to externally defined standards (Lester et al., 2016).

So, although specific expectations and practices in standards frameworks can help to address areas of concern and importance such as the complex knowledge and skills required to work with culturally and linguistically diverse learners (Santoro & Kennedy, 2016) or the nature of reflective practice in systems where this is mandated (Glasswell & Ryan, 2017), they can also create difficulties. A related criticism of standards frameworks lies in their a-contextuality, leading critics to observe that rather than being considered as a benchmark for professionalism, "some standards can obscure rather than recognise the complex questions about educational goals and directions which are at stake in the class-rooms" (Glasswell & Ryan, 2017, p. 24). Greater specificity or detail can also reflect a low level of trust in the profession, which leads to restricted agency, and more opportunities for concern about whether teachers are meeting standard expectations (Goodwin, 2021). Thus, while standards can provide consistency and credibility for the profession, the bulk of existing research in the area suggests that they can also lead to compliance and conformity (Call, 2020), a narrowing of innovative and creative practice and reduction in professional autonomy (Adoniou & Gallagher, 2017).

As shown in Table 8.1, several forms of teaching standards around the world present disciplinary knowledge as a core component of the professional work of teachers. It is logical to assume that a person engaged in teaching a subject would have a comprehensive knowledge of that subject to teach it effectively. However, a difficulty arises when teachers rely on standards to appraise their performance for the purposes of professional development and self-reflective evaluation. Standards can control the way the profession is measured and assessed, as well as the expected actions of teachers (van Dijk, 2015). They purport to represent a certain version of reality (Thomas, 2008), one characterised by non-specific expectations of efficacy, order, and respect. It is likely that the reasoning behind this is valid – no teaching context is the same, however, to narrowly prescribe expectations for teachers and teaching to a set of standards that are decontextualised and by definition, depersonalised, is problematic. Yet, educational policies that are designed to open and create space for localisation through unspecified standards of teacher quality can have

*Table 8.1* Examples of how disciplinary knowledge is cited in professional teaching standards

| Country | Standards statement |
| --- | --- |
| Australia (Australian Institute for Teaching and School Leadership, 2011) | Know the content and how to teach it |
| British Columbia, Canada (BC Teachers' Council, 2019) | Educators demonstrate a broad knowledge base and understanding of the areas they teach |
| Ireland (The Teaching Council, 2016) | "Subject knowledge and curriculum processes and content" is an element of professional knowledge and understanding |
| United States (National Board for Professional Teaching Standards, 2016) | Teachers know the subjects they teach and how to teach those subjects to students |
| United Kingdom (Education & Training Foundation, 2022) | Develop and update knowledge of your subject specialism taking account of new practices, research and/or industry requirements |

unintended consequences of further oppression (Rogers et al., 2005). Leaving the definition of *quality* open to individuals' interpretation runs the risk of creating preferential judgements, which may be made by colleagues in more senior roles, and/or based on different expectations. This tension is especially pertinent to ECTs, who are, by definition, often in hierarchical relationships managed by mentors/supervisors. For this reason, it is essential that the concept of teacher quality is better understood within the profession.

### Standards, early career teachers, and educational leadership: Uneasy transitions

For ECTs, the complexities inherent in the relationship between oversight through mandated standards, and their own expectations and emerging perceptions of professional autonomy can be particularly fraught. These tensions can impact negatively on their self-image, professional confidence and competence, and thus the way in which they enact their roles and practices in the school. The transition phase from ITE students to teaching professionals has been described by ECTs as being a 'lost at sea' or 'sink or swim' experience (Flores & Day, 2006; Stokking et al., 2003), with a workload that can lead to "pure exhaustion" (Schuck et al., 2018, p. 216), which may be mitigated by the school culture and relationships with colleagues. As Paniagua and Sánchez-Martí (2018) have observed, "the difficulties most ECTs encounter, which have largely remained unchanged over the last 50 years, are embedded characteristics of the teaching profession" (p. 4). Their early years can be fraught with challenges, that may lead to ECTs developing an identity as 'coping' (surviving) or 'managing' (thriving) (Hong et al., 2017), depending on the positive or negative environmental and contextual factors that support their progress.

As ECTs begin their professional journeys, they strive to make sense of their experiences, knowledge, and skills as they reconcile their preconceptions of what being a teacher means formed prior to their commencement in ITE programs with their lived experiences of teaching in the first years in the education profession (Morrison, 2013). This makes the early period in a teacher's career a productive time for exploration of how they are shaping up their professional identities as the teachers they are becoming, negotiating between person, context, and professional knowledge bases. During this time of transition, ECTs are claimed to develop a 'personal interpretive framework', a set of cognitions, motivations and beliefs that they use to give meaning as they react and respond to a variety of experiences, situations and conditions in the teaching environment (Keltchermans, 2019). They may develop their capacity to "exert influence, make choices, and take stances in ways that affect their work and/or their professional identities" (Eteläpelto et al., 2013, p. 61) allowing them opportunities to work through the frequent, routine occurrences and incidents that have been previously reported as the challenges and hurdles that have led to attrition. However, establishing a growing sense of self efficacy and agency in the early career phase for many teachers is likely to be mediated by performative measures, including compliance with professional teaching standards. This can lead to problems in creating a sustainable sense of identity (Simpson et al., 2018), 'psychic compliance' and potential burn-out and attrition (Moore & Clarke, 2016), as they continually work to "think, plan, and act in new ways" (Day, 2017, p. 174).

Although a lot of research has addressed issues of high attrition in ECTs leaving the profession in the first five years (Karsenti & Collin, 2013; Keltchermans, 2019), other recent research demonstrating the push-pull of factors leading mature teachers to leave the profession (Brandenburg et al., 2024) demonstrates the whole profession needs greater support. The education systems within which teachers work continue to grapple with issues of shortages and varying political, economic and social perceptions of teacher competency; if they are to succeed, teachers in all phases of their professional working lives must continue to question, reflect, and evolve to create and sustain supportive and viable career pathways for themselves. Identity formation is a fluid process and is negotiated by teachers through practice and influenced by the schooling context, their colleagues, the places and communities in which they teach, the roles they undertake, and the systemic policies and practices that shape the profession (Burke & Stets, 2023; Nichols et al., 2016). Behaving in ways consistent with role expectations outlined in the professional standards may heighten self-efficacy (Burke & Stets, 2023), but only where this does not conflict with teachers' deeper values and sense of purpose, and those of the schools in which they work. However, as much research internationally demonstrates, as ECTs are under great pressure to transition into a career while their identities are in the process of formation, they are thus highly likely to experience feelings of fragility and uncertainty.

Significant influences on them will include their understandings and experiences of induction into their school's teacher professional community (Beauchamp & Thomas, 2011), and their perceptions of the school leadership team, including the school principal. The impact of school leadership on teachers' sense of autonomy and well-being is strong (Toom, 2019). Understanding and acknowledging a teacher's motivation and commitment to their work is a valuable way for school leaders to support teacher performance and professional engagement (Han & Yin, 2016; Lambersky, 2016). Some school leaders will use the standards as a means of giving themselves, colleagues and ECTs' a sense of agency to develop into the kind of teacher they want to be (Buchanan, 2015) allowing their 'humanness' to emerge (Stets & Burke, 2014; Stets & Serpe,

2013). However, other school leaders may not, with this variability not being advantageous for the profession and sense making capabilities of ECTs as a group.

Rather than evaluating teacher performance in a binary way, determining if a teacher did or did not meet a particular standard, the indicators of teacher quality can be used by educators to negotiate the tension between their sense of professional identity, the teacher role prescribed by the standards, and the way they are translated into practice. Using the disciplinary knowledge example, encouraging teachers to reflect on not just what they know but what is known, and how they can increase their disciplinary understanding to engage in real perceptive and professional learning to further strengthen this and other knowledges is critical for sense-making and building teacher identity. Teachers can then begin to interact with standards and policies in a more meaningful way (Sachs, 2013; Torrance & Forde, 2017). Our research findings about teacher quality, in particular the Teacher Quality Construct, presents a pathway for teachers to rethink practice, their identities, and what it means to be a teacher in their schooling context.

## Navigating the tensions: Teacher quality and teaching standards

As part of the research process, the team focused in on three indicators of teacher quality that were identified by stakeholders as being of particular importance for ECTs: 1) motivation and commitment; 2) respect for diversity; and 3) reflective practice. The following section investigates these three qualities in depth, exploring the critical role of leaders in assisting teachers to utilise these aspects of the Teacher Quality Construct to enact and meaningfully enrich the content/skills heavy professional standards. To avoid the drift to what could be read as an explanation of isolated indicators, the discussion under each subsection continues to acknowledge the complex nature of teacher identity.

### *Motivation and commitment*

A teacher's motivation can be affected by their beliefs and expectations about the profession, how much they value teaching, what their goals are and how they set out to achieve them, and whether their motivation is intrinsic or extrinsic (Butler, 2007; Eyal & Roth, 2011; Watt & Richardson, 2015). Previous research has found that high teacher motivation and commitment to the profession can also lead to higher student achievement (Abazaoğlu & Aztekin, 2016), better job satisfaction, stronger sense of self-efficacy (Virtanen & Laine, 2021), more confident classroom management, and clarity of instruction (Irnidayanti et al., 2020). Motivation is at the heart of teacher decision making in relation to goals, expectations, and social and cognitive tasks (Hattie et al., 2020). What a teacher knows about their subject area, including specialist areas of knowledge, as well as new and evolving knowledge, and the ways in which the teacher communicates these to pupils are likely to be affected by the relative strength of their motivation. Motivation could explain why a music teacher knows less about contemporary K-pop and more about 1980s hair metal, or why a science teacher knows the periodic table better than the parts of a flower, or why a history teacher spends more time exploring ancient Egypt than Victorian era London. Teachers with a preference for working with certain age groups may be more motivated to understand the content and teaching strategies for those students over others.

In essence, this consideration of how teachers' motivation might influence content knowledge suggests that the way in which teachers are measured against this standard should go beyond what they do and do not know, and consider *why* they know what they know, and what that means for their work in context. Standards should acknowledge that *intrinsic motivation* in teachers is more likely to be associated with positive outcomes such as high performance and low burnout (Eyal & Roth, 2011). Facilitated reflection in this area could also lead to deeper exploration of what motivates teachers to teach in the first place, and how their current practice is congruent or dissonant with those motivations. Research also notes that a teacher's *commitment* to the profession can be affected by their personal concept of their teaching identity as well as the amount of support or mentoring they receive early in their career (Virtanen & Laine, 2021). Certain kinds of external pressures, such as systemic expectations for behaviour or results and a lack of mentoring and leadership support, can also affect a teacher's ability to be intrinsically motivated, leading to social and professional perceptions of inefficiency rather than effectiveness (Barni et al., 2019; De Clercq et al., 2022).


### *Respect for diversity*

To provide effective and meaningful teaching and learning for all students, it is vital for teachers to be able to understand, appreciate, and support the diverse community of students with whom they work daily. A twenty-first century teacher should be an interculturally competent professional who understands how to approach student differences in a positive way and effectively handle conflicts and conflict risks (Boghian, 2019). Diversity within a school community can include responding positively to factors such as "gender, cultural, ethnic, and First Nations identities; sexuality; rurality; family form; and socioeconomics" (Rowan et al., 2021, p. 149). To be a teacher who is respectful of diversity requires both cognitive and active engagement with the educational community and culture, and this would likely be reflected in the kind of content chosen to engage with and teach in their programs. For example, to have the broad knowledge base required of British Columbia teachers (BC Teachers' Council, 2019), or to be updating contemporary disciplinary knowledge to adhere to the UK standards (Education & Training Foundation, 2022), teachers need to understand and be critical of the different facets of their subject, including where knowledge comes from, how to navigate different perspectives on knowledge, and to know how to use diverse perspectives in the classroom in a meaningful and inclusive way. In doing so, such teachers utilise disciplinary content and student expertise and interest to create learners who "identify as citizens of the world" (Tichnor-Wagner et al., 2016, p. 26). Boon and Lewthwaite (2016) specifically termed this an 'ethic of care': "an ethical disposition that respects and values cultural diversity and uses cultural knowledge as a teaching tool" (p. 342). This positivity could be a result of broader cultural change in accepting learner diversity (Garrad et al., 2019), or be a purposeful development of the perspective that learner diversity is an enrichment to the classroom rather than a deficit (Bartolo & Smyth, 2009).

However, a study by Garrad et al. (2019), indicated that while, cognitively, teachers may be positive about inclusion and respectful engagement with diverse content and students, they may not be able to effectively follow this up with appropriate teaching and support strategies. In a series of multi-country case studies conducted by Herzog-Punzenberger et al. (2020), the practical effects of the positive attitudes of teachers towards culturally and linguistically diverse students were constrained by lack of resources, training and broader school support. Even if teachers are provided with adequate resources, with the lack of understanding and preparation, "it is doubtful that adapted curricula and resource material will directly impact classroom practice" (p. 416). As such, meeting standards related to content knowledge in a way that is inclusive and culturally responsive requires teachers to be supported by school leaders and systems through active support and professional learning.

### Reflective practice

Reflective practice is a core part of many teaching standards, indicating the importance it holds in the effective development of teachers across their careers. The National Board for Professional Teaching Standards in the United States emphasises that it is important for all teachers to understand the importance of continuous reflection and should commit to lifelong learning and reflection on practice (National Board for Professional Teaching Standards, 2016). Critical reflection is the primary component of the professional values in the UK standards (Education & Training Foundation, 2022) and is a part of continuous professional development in the standards for teachers in Pakistan (Pakistani Government Ministry of Education, 2009), Ireland (The Teaching Council, 2016), and Singapore (National Center on Education and the Economy, 2016), among others. For teachers to effectively know the content of their discipline and how to teach it, they need to reflect on all aspects of their practice, to understand what content is appropriate to cover, when, and with which students. Farrell (2020) posits that reflective practice is necessary for a teacher to "take more responsibility for their actions" (p. 277), by examining the theoretical and philosophical aspects of their practice. In doing so, they can question their beliefs and reasoning for their classroom practices and the content they choose to explore, developing resourcefulness, resilience, and professional responsibility for the pedagogical choices they make.

The act of reflection seems at first sight to be simple yet to be undertaken well it needs to take into account multiple factors. In practice it is demanding, since it involves the questioning or analysis of knowledge, skills as well as a teacher's actions. At its best, it is a form of thinking (Moon, 1999), "an active process that requires individuals to make the tacit explicit" (Mohamed et al., 2022, p. 6). Through reflection, teachers are able to examine their philosophies and principles of practice (Farrell, 2020), as well as their teaching environment, behaviours, personal competencies, and beliefs (Korthagen & Vasalos, 2005). This examination can occur during the teaching process (reflection-in-action) or after teaching has occurred (reflection-on-action) (Schön, 1983), with the overall purpose being for the educator to engage in some kind of change process. Gur-Ze'ev et al. (2001) cites 'transcendence' as the goal for reflection – to overcome history in some way and go beyond what is established or known. Whatever the focus of the reflection, reflective practices should lead to some kind of conceptual and/or practical change.

The role of management and leadership in supporting reflective processes through establishing optimal conditions is important. Careful consideration of practice can help strengthen teacher agency by allowing for deeper understanding of a context (Leijen et al., 2020), as well as increase emotional capital (a teacher's capacity to manage emotional resources in order to positively influence relationships and context) and foster collaboration with colleagues (Gkonou & Miller, 2021). Supervisors, or even more experienced colleagues, can help teachers develop their reflective practice by assisting with identifying valuable experiences for analysis, acting with empathy and acceptance, and helping to find and implement solutions (Korthagen & Vasalos, 2005).

## Conclusion: Shifting the discourse

This book has told the story of a major research study that initially sought to create and define a construct of teacher quality to inform a process for measuring the predictive validity of a TPA. As a result of the methodological design the project developed into a broader investigation into teacher identity and how the teaching profession could begin to measure all of what being a teacher encompasses. Our goal was to reposition the current deficit discourse around teacher quality by exemplifying a scholarly process to identify and measure what it values as indicators of teacher quality. We contend that the examination of *research informed teacher qualities* supports a positive reframing of the broader discourse around teacher quality. Our research acknowledges that the work of educators should be examined and subject to high expectations, but it should also allow for teachers to be trusted to reflect on their practice in context and have the agency to consider the relationship between self and a standardised role.

The use of professional standards in teaching is a complex issue that requires ongoing engagement from educators to prevent 'standards' from being objectivised, becoming an unequivocal means of judging teachers and their capacity to teach. Only addressing the dimension of teaching, the skills, knowledge and actions necessary for appropriate professional conduct, leads teachers to constantly focus on what they do, rather than what being a teacher means and why they are teaching in particular ways. Knowledge and actions do not exist in a vacuum; who a teacher is matters just as much as what they do. Without acknowledging context and giving weight to teacher qualities that go beyond teaching, knowledge and skills, teachers will continue to feel personally devalued and burn out early. Utilising indicators of teacher quality to interpret and examine standards and professional practice is one way for teachers and school leaders to develop an understanding of how their qualities impact their ability to meet the relevant professional standards and utilise strategies specific to their needs to better assess and develop their skills. For a teacher to understand the content of their discipline, it means a teacher needs to be motivated to understand and explore the breadth of the subject, to actively pursue and represent a diverse range of perspectives and reflect on and improve knowledge deficits to better serve their students. Making this relationship between who teachers are and the work that they do more explicit gives professional standards more contextual meaning, enhances nuanced understandings of teachers and teaching, and celebrates the complexity.

The Teacher Quality Construct components and indicators could contribute to deeper teacher understanding and reflection on practice to more effectively meet the standards. A teacher's level of initiative or curiosity may influence their capacity to pursue new and unusual areas of content knowledge or to be engaged in whole school initiatives and strategies. A teacher's perceived self-efficacy may explain why they are more or less reluctant to delve into new content that they have no experience in teaching. A teacher's patience levels may even affect their capacity to pursue difficult or complex content in depth or explore making connections with content in other learning areas that may engage students or enhance their learning. Considering these aspects of what it means to be a teacher shifts the conversation away from what educators do and do not know, and into more meaningful discussions of why and how they teach what they teach. In doing so, it opens pathways for recognition and purposeful development of qualities that can have a real impact on practice and professional engagement. Examining the qualities that relate to a teacher's identity can lead to a more comprehensive and agentic understanding of self and role, while in pursuit of more comprehensive content knowledge.

The findings from the WtE study show that it is vital to enable educators, from early career through to school leadership, to engage in the necessary work to navigate the tensions between teacher role, teacher identity, and teacher quality within the broad contexts of external mandates, school cultures, and their own understandings of what it means to be a teacher. Shifting the discourse from what teachers do to include who teachers are enables more nuanced conversations about the fluid and multidimensional nature of teacher identity formation, broadens the potential scope of professional standards for effective teacher development, and allows teachers to reflect on their capacity for productive and influential pedagogy. We advocate for research and practice to continue the conversation by investigating and supporting teacher quality, to help make sense of the challenging, unpredictable educational landscapes of teachers' worlds.

## Key References

Adoniou, M., & Gallagher, M. (2017). Professional standards for teachers – what are they good for? *Oxford Review of Education, 43*(1), 109–126. https://doi.org/10.1080/03054985.2016.1243522

Connolly, M., James, C., & Fertig, M. (2019). The difference between educational management and educational leadership and the importance of educational responsibility. *Educational Management Administration & Leadership, 47*(4), 504–519. https://doi.org/10.1177/1741143217745880

Herzog-Punzenberger, B., Altrichter, H., Brown, M., Burns, D., Nortvedt, G. A., Skedsmo, G., Wiese, E., Nayir, F., Fellner, M., McNamara, G., & O'Hara, J. (2020). Teachers responding to cultural diversity: Case studies on assessment practices, challenges and experiences in secondary schools in Austria, Ireland, Norway and Turkey. *Educational Assessment, Evaluation and Accountability, 32*, 395–424. https://doi.org/10.1007/s11092-020-09330-y

Hong, J., Day, C., & Greene, B. (2017). The construction of early career teachers' identities: Coping or managing? *Teacher Development, 22*(2), 249–266. https://doi.org/10.1080/13664530.2017.1403367

Keltchermans, G. (2019). Early career teachers and their need for support: Thinking again. In A. Sullivan, B. Johnson, & M. Simons (Eds.), *Attracting and keeping the best teachers: Professional learning and development in schools and high education* (Vol. 16). Springer. https://doi.org/10.1007/978-981-13-8621-3_5

Sachs, J. (2016). Teacher professionalism: Why are we still talking about it? *Teachers and Teaching, 22*(4), 413–425. https://doi.org/10.1080/13540602.2015.1082732

Watt, H. M. G., & Richardson, P. W. (2015). Teacher motivation. In J. D. Wright (Ed.), *International encyclopedia of the social & behavioral sciences* (2nd ed.). (pp. 64–71). Elsevier. https://doi.org/10.1016/B978-0-08-097086-8.26082-0

# References


Abazaoğlu, İ., & Aztekin, S. (2016). The role of teacher morale and motivation on students' science and math achievement: Findings from Singapore, Japan, Finland and Turkey. *Universal Journal of Educational Research, 4*(11), 2606–2617. https://doi.org/10.13189/ujer.2016.041114

Acocella, I. (2012). The focus groups in social research: Advantages and disadvantages. *Quality & Quantity, 46,* 1125–1136. https://doi.org/10.1007/s11135-011-9600-4

Aditomo, A., & Köhler, C. (2020). Do student ratings provide reliable and valid information about teaching quality at the school level? Evaluating measures of science teaching in PISA 2015. *Educational Assessment, Evaluation and Accountability, 32*(3), 275–310. https://doi.org/10.1007/s11092-020-09328-6

Admiraal, W., & Kittelsen Røberg, K.-I. (2023). Teachers' job demands, resources and their job satisfaction: Satisfaction with school, career choice and teaching profession of teachers in different career stages. *Teaching and Teacher Education, 125,* Article 104063. https://doi.org/10.1016/j.tate.2023.104063

Admiraal, W., Kittelsen Røberg, K.-I., Wiers-Jenssen, J., & Saab, N. (2023). Mind the gap: Early-career teachers' level of preparedness, professional development, working conditions, and feelings of distress. *Social Psychology of Education, 26,* 1759–1787.

Ahmad, K. B., & Kutty, F. B. M. (2023). The influence of self-resilience and self-belief on teachers' choice of coping strategies in the workplace. *International Journal of Academic Research in Progressive Education and Development, 12*(3), 568–587. https://doi.org/10.6007/IJARPED/v12-i3/18462

Ainsworth, S., & Oldfield, J. (2019). Quantifying teacher resilience: Context matters. *Teaching and Teacher Education, 82,* 117–128. https://doi.org/10.1016/j.tate.2019.03.012

Akkerman, S. F., & Meijer, P. C. (2011). A dialogical approach to conceptualizing teacher identity. *Teaching and Teacher Education, 27,* 308–319. https://doi.org/10.1016/j.tate.2010.08.013

Alake-Tuenter, E., Biemans, H. J. A., Tobi, H., & Mulder, M. (2013). Inquiry-based science teaching competence of primary school teachers: A Delphi study. *Teaching and Teacher Education, 35,* 13–24. https://doi.org/10.1016/j.tate.2013.04.013

Almujlli, G., Alrabah, R., Al-Ghosen, A., & Munshi, F. (2022). Conducting virtual focus groups during the COVID-19 epidemic utilizing videoconferencing technology: A feasibility study. *Cureus, 14*(3), Article e23540. https://doi.org/10.7759/cureus.23540

Alzobiani, I. (2020). The qualities of effective teachers as perceived by Saudi EFL students and teachers. *English Language Teaching, 13*(2), 32–47. https://doi.org/10.5539/elt.v13n2p32

American Educational Research Association, American Psychological Association, & National Council on Measurement in Education. (1999). *Standards for educational and psychological testing.* American Educational Research Association. https://www.aera.net/Portals/38/1999%20Standards_revised.pdf

American Educational Research Association, American Psychological Association, & National Council on Measurement in Education. (2014). *Standards for educational and psychological testing.* American Educational Research Association. https://www.testingstandards.net/uploads/7/6/6/4/76643089/standards_2014edition.pdf

Amitai, A., & Van Houtte, M. (2022). Being pushed out of the career: Former teachers' reasons for leaving the profession. *Teaching and Teacher Education, 110*, Article 103540. https://doi.org/10.1016/j.tate.2021.103540

Anderson, S., Allen, P., Peckham, S., & Goodwin, N. (2008). Asking the right questions: Scoping studies in the commissioning of research on the organisation and delivery of health services. *Health Research Policy and Systems, 6*, Article 7. https://doi.org/10.1186/1478-4505-6-7

Angoff, W. H. (1971). Scales, norms, and equivalent scores. In R. L. Thorndike (Ed.), *Educational measurement* (2nd ed., pp. 508–600). American Council on Education.

Appel, M. (2020). Performativity and the demise of the teaching profession: The need for rebalancing in Australia. *Asia-Pacific Journal of Teacher Education, 48*(3), 301–315. https://doi.org/10.1080/1359866X.2019.1644611

Armstrong, R., Hall, B., Doyle, J., & Waters, E. (2011). 'Scoping the scope' of a Cochrane review. *Journal of Public Health, 33*(1), 147–150. https://doi.org/10.1093/pubmed/fdr015

Australian Government Department of Education. (2022). *National teacher workforce action plan.* https://www.education.gov.au/national-teacher-workforce-action-plan

Australian Government Productivity Commission. (2022). *Review of the National School Reform Agreement: Study report.* https://www.pc.gov.au/inquiries/completed/school-agreement/report/school-agreement-overview.pdf

Australian Institute for Teaching and School Leadership. (2011). *Australian professional standards for teachers.* https://www.aitsl.edu.au/standards

Australian Institute for Teaching and School Leadership. (2022). *Building a culturally responsive Australian teaching workforce: Final report for Indigenous cultural competency project.* https://www.aitsl.edu.au/docs/default-source/comms/cultural-competency/aitsl_indigenous-cultural-competency_final-report_.pdf

Avella, J. R. (2016). Delphi panels: Research design, procedures, advantages, and challenges. *International Journal of Doctoral Studies*, *11*, 305–321. https://doi.org/10.28945/3561

Bahadir, F., & Tuncer, M. (2020). Determining the standards of teaching and learning process as a component of curriculum. *International Journal of Progressive Education*, *16*(3), 34–52. https://doi.org/10.29329/ijpe.2020.248.3

Bailes, L. P., & Nandakumar, R. (2020). Get the most from your survey: An application of Rasch analysis for education leaders. *International Journal of Education Policy and Leadership*, *16*(2). https://doi.org/10.22230/ijepl.2020v16n2a857

Ball, H. L. (2019). Conducting online surveys. *Journal of Human Lactation*, *35*(3), 413–417. https://doi.org/10.1177/0890334419848734

Ball, S. J. (2003). The teacher's soul and the terrors of performativity. *Journal of Education Policy*, *18*(2), 215–228. https://doi.org/10.1080/0268093022000043065

Banks, J. A. (2015). *Cultural diversity and education: Foundations, curriculum, and teaching* (6th ed.). Routledge. https://doi.org/10.4324/9781315622255

Bardach, L., & Klassen, R. M. (2020). Smart teachers, successful students? A systematic review of the literature on teachers' cognitive abilities and teacher effectiveness. *Educational Research Review*, *30*, Article 100312. https://doi.org/10.1016/j.edurev.2020.100312

Barni, D., Danioni, F., & Benevene, P. (2019). Teachers' self-efficacy: The role of personal values and motivations for teaching. *Frontiers in Psychology*, *10*, Article 1645. https://doi.org/10.3389/fpsyg.2019.01645

Barrios, M., Guilera, G., Nuño, L., & Gómez-Benito, J. (2021). Consensus in the Delphi method: What makes a decision change? *Technological Forecasting and Social Change*, *163*, Article 120484. https://doi.org/10.1016/j.techfore.2020.120484

Bartolo, P., & Smyth, G. (2009). Teacher education for diversity. In A. Swennen & M. van der Klink (Eds.), *Becoming a teacher educator: Theory and practice for teacher educators* (pp. 117–132). Springer. https://doi.org/10.1007/978-1-4020-8874-2_9

BC Teachers' Council. (2019). *Professional standards for BC educators*. https://www2.gov.bc.ca/assets/gov/education/kindergarten-to-grade-12/teach/teacher-regulation/standards-for-educators/edu_standards.pdf

Beauchamp, C., & Thomas, L. (2011). New teachers' identity shifts at the boundary of teacher education and initial practice. *International Journal of Educational Research*, *50*, 6–13. https://doi.org/10.1016/j.ijer.2011.04.003

Beauchamp, G., Clarke, L., Hulme, M., & Murray, J. (2015). Teacher education in the United Kingdom post devolution: convergences and divergences. *Oxford Review of Education*, *41*(2), 154–170. https://doi.org/10.1080/03054985.2015.1017403

Beijaard, D., & Meijer, P. C. (2017). Developing the personal and professional in making a teacher identity. In D. J. Clandinin & J. Husu (Eds.),

*The SAGE handbook of research on teacher education.* (pp. 177–192). SAGE.

Beltmann, S., Mansfield, C., and Price, A. (2011). Thriving not just surviving: A review of research on teacher resilience. *Educational Research Review, 6*, 185–207. https://doi.org/10.1016/j.edurev.2011.09.001

Bennett, J., Tognolini, J., & Pickering, S. (2012). Establishing and applying performance standards for curriculum-based examinations. *Assessment in Education: Principles, Policy & Practice, 19*(3), 321–339. https://doi.org/10.1080/0969594X.2011.614219

Bennett, R., Demmers, T. A., Plourde, H., Arrey, K., Armour, B., Ferland, G., & Kakinami, L. (2019). Identifying barriers of arthritis-related disability on food behaviors to guide nutrition interventions. *Journal of Nutrition Education and Behavior, 51*(9), 1058–1066. https://doi.org/10.1016/j.jneb.2019.06.030

Bennett, R. E. (2015). The changing nature of educational assessment. *Review of Research in Education, 39*(1), 370–407. https://doi.org/10.3102/0091732x14554179

Bennett, R. E. (2019). Integrating measurement principles into formative assessment. In H. L. Andrade, R. E. Bennett, & G. J. Cizek (Eds.), *Handbook of formative assessment in the disciplines* (pp. 20–31). Routledge.

Berk, R. A. (2012). Top 20 strategies to increase the online response rates of student rating scales. *International Journal of Technology in Teaching & Learning, 8*(2), 98–107.

Beykont, Z. F. (2013). Building a well-prepared languages teaching force: Turkish teacher perspectives. *Babel, 47* (3), 16+. https://link.gale.com/apps/doc/A335734055/AONE?

Biçer, N., & Batdı, V. (2019). An investigation of textbooks used to teach Turkish as a foreign language with Rasch measurement model and Maxqda. *Journal of Language and Linguistic Studies, 15*(4), 1269–1286. https://doi.org/10.17263/jlls.668420

Biesta, G., Priestly, M., & Robinson, S. (2015). The role of beliefs in teacher agency. *Teachers and Teaching, 21*(6), 624–640. https://doi.org/10.1080/13540602.2015.1044325

Bigham, S. G., Hively, D. E., & Toole, G. H. (2014). Principals' and cooperating teachers' expectations of teacher candidates. *Education, 135*(2), 211–229.

Black, D., Hine, G., & Lavery, S. (2023). Exploring challenges faced by early career primary school teachers: A qualitative study. *Australian Journal of Teacher Education, 48*(8), Article 1. https://doi.org/10.14221/1835-517X.6147

Boghian, I. (2019). Empowering teachers to deal with classroom diversity. *Revista Românească pentru Educaţie Multidimensională, 11*(3), 1–10. https://doi.org/10.18662/rrem/134

Bond, T. G., & Fox, C. M. (2007). *Applying the Rasch model: Fundamental measurement in the human sciences* (2nd ed.). Lawrence Erlbaum Associates.

Bond, T. G., Yan, Z., & Heene, M. (2020). *Applying the Rasch model: Fundamental measurement in the human sciences* (4th ed.). Routledge. https://doi.org/10.4324/9780429030499

Bonner, P. J., Warren, S. R., & Jiang, Y. H. (2018). Voices from urban classrooms: Teachers' perceptions on instructing diverse students and using culturally responsive teaching. *Education and Urban Society, 50*(8), 697–726. https://doi.org/10.1177/0013124517713820

Boon, H. J., & Lewthwaite, B. E. (2016). Teacher ethics: The link between quality teaching and multi-ethnic and multiracial education. *Athens Journal of Education, 3*(4), 331–344. https://doi.org/10.30958/aje.3-4-3

Brandenburg, R., Larsen, E., Simpson, A., Sallis, R., & Tran, D. (2024). 'I left the teaching profession... and this is what I am doing now': A national study of teacher attrition. *Australian Educational Researcher, 51*, 2381–2400. https://doi.org/10.1007/s13384-024-00697-1

Braun, V., & Clarke, V. (2022). Conceptual and design thinking for thematic analysis. *Qualitative Psychology, 9*(1), 3–26. https://doi.org/10.1037/qup0000196

Braun, H. I., Jackson, D. N., Messick, S., & Wiley, D. E. (2001). *The role of constructs in psychological and educational measurement*. Routledge. https://doi.org/10.4324/9781410607454

Brookhart, S. M., & Chen, F. (2015). The quality and effectiveness of descriptive rubrics. *Educational Review, 67*(3), 343–368. https://doi.org/10.1080/00131911.2014.929565

Buchanan, R. (2015). Teacher identity and agency in an era of accountability. *Teachers and Teaching, 21*(6), 700–719. https://doi.org/10.1080/13540602.2015.1044329

Burke, P. J., & Stets, J. E. (2023). *Identity theory* (2nd ed.). Oxford University Press. https://doi.org/1093/oso/9780197617182.003.0003

Butler, R. (2007). Teachers' achievement goal orientations and associations with teachers' help seeking: Examination of a novel approach to teacher motivation. *Journal of Educational Psychology, 99*(2), 241–252. https://doi.org/10.1037/0022-0663.99.2.241

Call, K. (2020). Impacts of professional standards on teacher education. In M. A. Peters (Ed.), *Encyclopedia of teacher education* (pp. 790–795). Springer Nature. https://doi.org/10.1007/978-981-16-8679-5

Cascio, M. A., Lee, E., Vaudrin, N., & Freedman, D. A. (2019). A team-based approach to open coding: Considerations for creating intercoder consensus. *Field Methods, 31*(2), 116–130. https://doi.org/10.1177/1525822X19838237

Casely-Hayford, J., Björklund, C., Bergström, G., Lindqvist, P., & Kwak, L. (2022). What makes teachers stay? A cross-sectional exploration of the individual and contextual factors associated with teacher retention in Sweden. *Teaching and Teacher Education, 113*, Article 103664. https://doi.org/10.1016/j.tate.2022.103664

Chavez, V. (2012, August 9). *Cultural humility: People, principles and practice* [Video]. Youtube. https://www.youtube.com/watch?v=SaSHLbS1V4w

Check, J., & Schutt, R. K. (2011). *Research methods in education*. SAGE. https://doi.org/10.4135/9781544307725

Chetty, R., Friedman, J. N., & Rockoff, J. E. (2014). Measuring the impacts of teachers II: Teacher value-added and student outcomes in adulthood. *American Economic Review, 104*(9), 2633–2679. https://doi.org/10.1257/aer.104.9.2633

Chowdhury, M. (2018). Emphasizing morals, values, ethics, and character education in science education and science teaching. *MOJES: Malaysian Online Journal of Educational Science, 4*(2), 1–16. https://files.eric.ed.gov/fulltext/EJ1095995.pdf

Chu, X., Ilyas, I. F., Krishnan, S., & Wang, J. (2016). Data cleaning: Overview and emerging challenges. In *SIGMOD '16: Proceedings of the 2016 International Conference on Management of Data* (pp. 2201–2206). Association for Computing Machinery. https://doi.org/10.1145/2882903.2912574

Claessens, B., van Eerde, W., Rutte, C. G., & Roe, R. A. (2007). A review of the time management literature. *Personnel Review, 36*(2), 255–276. https://doi.org/10.1108/00483480710726136

Cochran-Smith, M. (2001). The outcomes question in teacher education. *Teaching and Teacher Education, 17*(5), 527–546. https://doi.org/10.1016/S0742-051X(01)00012-9

Cochran-Smith, M., & Fries, K. (2005). The AERA panel on research and teacher education: Context and goals. In M. Cochran-Smith & K. M. Zeichner (Eds.), *Studying teacher education: The report of the AERA panel on research and teacher education* (pp. 37–68). Lawrence Erlbaum Associates. http://ereserve.library.utah.edu/Annual/ECS/6605/Thompson/researchon.pdf

Collie, R. J., Shapka, J. D., Perry, N. E., & Martin, A. J. (2016). Teachers' psychological functioning in the workplace: Exploring the roles of contextual beliefs, need satisfaction, and personal characteristics. *Journal of Educational Psychology, 108*(6), 788–799. https://doi.org/10.1037/edu0000088

Connell, R. (2009). Good teachers on dangerous ground: Towards a new view of teacher quality and professionalism. *Critical Studies in Education, 50*(3), 213–229. https://doi.org/10.1080/17508480902998421

Cooper, K., & Olson, M. (1996). The multiple 'I's' of teacher identity. In T. Boak, R. Bond, D. Dworet, & M. Kompf (Eds.), *Changing research and practice: Teachers' professionalism, identities and knowledge* (pp. 78–89). Routledge.

Craven, G., Beswick, K., Fleming, J., Fletcher, T., Green, M., Jensen, B., Leinonen, E., & Rickards, F. (2014). *Action now: Classroom ready teachers*. Teacher Education Ministerial Advisory Group. https://www.aitsl.edu.au/tools-resources/resource/action-now-classroom-ready-teachers

Crocker, L., & Algina, J. (1986). *Introduction to classical and modern test theory*. Holt, Rinehart, and Winston.

Cronbach, L. J. (1990). *Essentials of psychological testing* (5th ed.). HarperCollins.

Custer, R. L., Scarcella, J. A., & Stewart, B. R. (1999). The modified Delphi technique – A rotational modification. *Journal of Career and Technical Education, 15*(2), 50–58. https://doi.org/10.21061/jcte.v15i2.702

Dalkey, N., & Helmer, O. (1963). An experimental application of the Delphi method to the use of experts. *Management Science, 9*(3), 458–467. https://doi.org/10.1287/mnsc.9.3.458

Darling-Hammond, L. (2000). Teacher quality and student achievement. *Education Policy Analysis Archives, 8,* 1–44. https://doi.org/10.14507/epaa.v8n1.2000

Darling-Hammond, L. (2012). The right start: Creating a strong foundation for the teaching career. *Phi Delta Kappan, 94*(3), 8–13. https://doi.org/10.1177/003172171209400303

Darling-Hammond, L., & Richardson, N. (2009). Teacher learning: What matters? *Educational Leadership, 66*(5), 46–53.

Darling-Hammond, L., Wise, A. E., & Klein, S. P. (1995). *A license to teach: Building a profession for 21st-century schools.* Routledge.

Davis, J. L., Love, T. P., & Fares, P. (2019). Collective social identity: Synthesizing identity theory and social identity theory using digital data. *Social Psychology Quarterly, 82*(3), 254–273. https://doi.org/10.1177/0190272519851025

Davis, K., Drey, N., & Gould, D. (2009). What are scoping studies? A review of the nursing literature. *International Journal of Nursing Studies, 46*(10), 1386–1400. https://doi.org/10.1016/j.ijnurstu.2009.02.010

Day, C. (2017). *Teachers' worlds and work: Understanding complexity, building quality.* Routledge. https://doi.org/10.4324/9780203578490

De Clercq, M., Watt, H. M., & Richardson, P. W. (2022). Profiles of teachers' striving and wellbeing: Evolution and relations with context factors, retention, and professional engagement. *Journal of Educational Psychology, 114*(3), 637–649. https://doi.org/10.1037/edu0000702

Denofrio, L. A., Russell, B., Lopatto, D., & Lu, Y. (2007). Linking student interests to science curricula. *Science, 318,* 1872–1873. https://doi.org/10.1126/science.1150788

Dille, K. B., & Røkenes, F. M. (2021). Teachers' professional development in formal online communities: A scoping review. *Teaching and Teacher Education, 105,* Article 103431. https://doi.org/10.1016/j.tate.2021.103431

Dinham, S. (2016). *Leading learning and teaching.* ACER Press.

Doda, N., & Knowles, T. (2008). Listening to the voices of young adolescents. *Middle School Journal, 39*(3), 26–33. https://doi.org/10.1080/00940771.2008.11461630

Doll, B., Zucker, S., & Brehm, K. (2004). *Resilient classrooms: Creating healthy environments for learning.* Guilford Publications.

Donker, M. H., van Vemde, L., Hessen, D. J., van Gog, T., & Mainhard, T. (2021). Observational, student, and teacher perspectives on interpersonal teacher behavior: Shared and unique associations with teacher and student emotions. *Learning and Instruction, 73,* Article 101414. https://doi.org/10.1016/j.learninstruc.2020.101414

Drisko, J., & Maschi, T. (2015). *Content analysis.* Oxford University Press. https://doi.org/10.1093/acprof:oso/9780190215491.001.0001

Duggleby, W. (2005). What about focus group interaction data? *Qualitative Health Research, 15*(6), 832–840. https://doi.org/10.1177/1049732304273916

Eckert, J., Ulmer, J., Khachatryan, E., & Ledesma, P. (2016). Career pathways of teacher leaders in the United States: Adding and path-finding new professional roles. *Professional Development in Education, 42*(5), 687–709. https://doi.org/10.1080/19415257.2015.1084644

Education & Training Foundation. (2022). *Professional standards for teachers and trainers in the further education and training sector.* https://www.et-foundation.co.uk/wp-content/uploads/2022/04/PS-for-Teachers_Summary-of-Standards_A4-Poster_Final.pdf

Egan, K. L., Schneider, M. C., & Ferrara, S. (2012). Performance level descriptors: History, practice, and a proposed framework. In G. J. Cizek (Ed.), *Setting performance standards foundations, methods, and innovations* (2nd ed., pp. 79–106). Lawrence Erlbaum Associates.

Eisner, E. (1979). *The educational imagination: On the design and evaluation of school programs.* Macmillan.

Eteläpelto, A., Vähäsantanen, K., Hökkä, P., & Paloniemi, S. (2013). What is agency? Conceptualizing professional agency at work. *Educational Research Review, 10*, 45–65. https://doi.org/10.1016/j.edurev.2013.05.001

Evans, C. (2008). The effectiveness of m-learning in the form of podcast revision lectures in higher education. *Computers & Education, 50*(2), 491–498. https://doi.org/10.1016/j.compedu.2007.09.016

Eyal, O., & Roth, G. (2011). Principals' leadership and teachers' motivation: Self-determination theory analysis. *Journal of Educational Administration, 49*(3), 256–275. https://doi.org/10.1108/09578231111129055

Farrell, T. S. C. (2020). Professional development through reflective practice for English-medium instruction (EMI) teachers. *International Journal of Bilingual Education and Bilingualism, 23*(3), 277–286. https://doi.org/10.1080/13670050.2019.1612840

Fauth, B., Decristan, J., Decker, A.-T., Büttner, G., Hardy, I., Klieme, E., & Kunter, M. (2019). The effects of teacher competence on student outcomes in elementary science education: The mediating role of teaching quality. *Teaching and Teacher Education, 86*, Article 102882. https://doi.org/10.1016/j.tate.2019.102882

Federičová, M. (2021). Teacher turnover: What can we learn from Europe? *European Journal of Education, 56*(1), 102–116. https://doi.org/10.1111/ejed.12429

Fetherston, T., & Lummis, G. (2012). Why Western Australian secondary teachers resign. *Australian Journal of Teacher Education, 37*(4), Article 1. https://doi.org/10.14221/ajte.2012v37n4.1

Fletcher, A. J., & Marchildon, G. P. (2014). Using the Delphi method for qualitative, participatory action research in health leadership. *International Journal of Qualitative Methods, 13*(1), 1–18. https://doi.org/10.1177/160940691401300101

Flores, M. A. (2011). Teachers' work and lives: A European perspective. In C. Day (Ed.), *The Routledge international handbook of teacher and school development* (pp. 94–107). Routledge.

Flores, M. A. (2016). Teacher education curriculum. In J. Loughran & M. L. Hamilton (Eds.), *International handbook of teacher education* (Vol. 1, pp. 187–230). Springer.

Flores, M. A., & Day, C. (2006). Contexts which shape and reshape new teachers' identities: A multi-perspective study. *Teaching and Teacher Education*, *22*(2), 219–232. https://doi.org/10.1016/j.tate.2005.09.002

Forde, C., McMahon, M. A., Hamilton, G., & Murray, R. (2016). Rethinking professional standards to promote professional learning. *Professional Development in Education*, *42*(1), 19–35. https://doi.org/10.1080/19415257.2014.999288

Frye, K. E., Garis, E. J., Myers, T. O., Huggins-Manley, A. C., Smith-Bonahue, T. M., Kemple, K. M., & Kehl, L. (2024). Reliability and validity evidence for an adapted affect knowledge test for preschool children using Rasch theory. *Early Education and Development*, 36(2), 1–24. https://doi.org/10.1080/10409289.2024.2389369

Fu, G., & Clarke, A. (2019). Teachers' moral agency under neo-liberal influences: What is educationally desirable in China's curriculum reform? *Educational Review*, *71*(1), 51–66. https://doi.org/10.1080/0013 1911.2019.1524205

Galavi, Z., & Khajouei, R. (2023). Online focus groups for the development of a usability evaluation tool: Lessons learned. *Frontiers in Health Informatics*, *12*, Article 154. https://doi.org/10.30699/fhi.v12i0.483

García, E., Han, E. S., & Weiss, E. (2022). Determinants of teacher attrition: Evidence from district-teacher matched data. *Education Policy Analysis Archives*, *30*(25). https://doi.org/10.14507/epaa.30.6642

García, E., & Weiss, E. (2019). *The teacher shortage is real, large and growing, and worse than we thought: The first report in 'The Perfect Storm in the Teacher Labor Market' series*. Economic Policy Institute. https://files.epi.org/pdf/163651.pdf

Garrad, T.-A., Rayner, C., & Pedersen, S. (2019). Attitudes of Australian primary school teachers towards the inclusion of students with autism spectrum disorders. *Journal of Research in Special Educational Needs*, *19*(1), 58–67. https://doi.org/10.1111/1471-3802.12424

Gilflores, J., & Alonso, C. G. (1995). Using focus groups in educational research: Exploring teachers' perspectives on educational change. *Evaluation Review*, *19*(1), 84–101. https://doi.org/10.1177/0193841X950 1900104

Gilmore, B., & Kramer, M. W. (2019). We are who we say we are: Teachers' shared identity in the workplace. *Communication Education*, *68*(1), 1–19. https://doi.org/10.1080/03634523.2018.1536271

Girgin, D. (2020). An investigation of the songs created by student-teachers in music via an Interdisciplinary approach based on the Rasch measurement model and the Maxqda analysis program. *International Online Journal of Education and Teaching*, *7*(4), 1661–1687. https://files.eric.ed.gov/fulltext/EJ1271097.pdf

Gkonou, C., & Miller, E. R. (2021). An exploration of language teacher reflection, emotion labour, and emotional capita. *TESOL Quarterly*, *55*(1), 134–155. https://doi.org/10.1002/tesq.580

Glasswell, K., & Ryan, J. (2017). Reflective practice in teacher professional standards: Reflection as mandatory practice. In R. Brandenburg, K. Glasswell, M. Jones, & J. Ryan (Eds.), *Reflective theory and practice in teacher education* (pp. 3–26). Springer. https://doi.org/10.1007/978-981-10-3431-2_1

Goepel, J. (2012). Upholding public trust: An examination of teacher professionalism and the use of teachers' standards in England. *Teacher Development, 16*(4), 489–505. https://doi.org/10.1080/13664530.2012.729784

Goodfellow, L. T. (2023). An overview of survey research. *Respiratory Care, 68*(9), 1309–1313. https://doi.org/10.4187/respcare.11041

Goodwin, A. L. (2021). Teaching standards, globalisation, and conceptions of teacher professionalism. *European Journal of Teacher Education, 44*(1), 5–19. https://doi.org/10.1080/02619768.2020.1833855

Goodwin, A. L., Lee, C. C., & Pratt, S. (2023). The poetic humanity of teacher education: Holistic mentoring for beginning teachers. *Professional Development in Education, 49*(4), 707–724. https://doi.org/10.1080/19415257.2021.1973067

Goodwin, A. L., Low, E. L., & Ng, P. T. (2015). Developing teacher leadership in Singapore: Multiple pathways for differential journeys. *The New Educator, 11*(2), 107–120. https://doi.org/10.1080/1547688X.2015.1026782

Grant, M. J., & Booth, A. (2009). A typology of reviews: An analysis of 14 review types and associated methodologies. *Health Information & Libraries Journal, 26*(2), 91–108. https://doi.org/10.1111/j.1471-1842.2009.00848.x

Gratacós, G., Mena, J., & Ciesielkiewicz, M. (2023). The complexity thinking approach: Beginning teacher resilience and perceived self-efficacy as determining variables in the induction phase. *European Journal of Teacher Education, 46*(2), 331–348. https://doi.org/10.1080/02619768.2021.1900113

Greatorex, J. (2003). Developing and applying level descriptors. *Westminster Studies in Education, 26*(2), 125–133. https://doi.org/10.1080/0140672030260205

Green, R. A. (2014). The Delphi technique in educational research. *SAGE Open, 4*(2). https://doi.org/10.1177/2158244014529773

Guba, E. G. (1981). Criteria for assessing the trustworthiness of naturalistic inquiries. *ECTJ, 29*(2), 75–91. https://doi.org/10.1007/BF02766777

Gur-Ze'ev, I., Masschelein, J., & Blake, N. (2001). Reflectivity, reflection, and counter-education. *Studies in Philosophy and Education, 20*, 93–106. https://doi.org/10.1023/A:1010303001871

Haag, S., & Megowan-Romanowicz, C. (2015). Next generation science standards: A national mixed-methods study on teacher readiness. *School Science & Mathematics, 115*, 416–426. https://doi.org/10.1111/ssm.12145

Haddix, M. M. (2015). *Cultivating racial and linguistic diversity in literacy teacher education*. Routledge. https://doi.org/10.4324/9781315850665

Han, J., & Yin, H. (2016). Teacher motivation: Definition, research development and implications for teachers. *Cogent Education, 3*(1), Article 1217819 https://doi.org/10.1080/2331186X.2016.1217819

Hanushek, E., & Rivkin, S. (2006). Teacher quality. In E. Hanushek & F. Welch (Eds.), *Handbook of the economics of education* (Vol. 2, pp. 1051–1078). Elsevier. https://doi.org/10.1016/S1574-0692(06)02018-6

Hanushek, E. A., Kain, J. F., O'Brien, D. M., & Rivkin, S. G. (2005). *The market for teacher quality* [Working Paper No. 11154]. https://doi.org/10.3386/w11154

Hargreaves, A., & Braun, H. (2013). *Data-driven improvement and accountability*. National Education Policy Center.

Harlow, A. (2010). Online surveys – Possibilities, pitfalls and practicalities: The experience of the TELA evaluation. *Waikato Journal of Education, 15*(2). https://doi.org/10.15663/wje.v15i2.116

Harris, A., & Jones, M. (2020). COVID 19 – School leadership in disruptive times. *School Leadership & Management, 40*(4), 243–247. https://doi.org/10.1080/13632434.2020.1811479

Harris, D. N., & Sass, T. R. (2011). Teacher training, teacher quality and student achievement. *Journal of Public Economics, 95*, 798–812. https://doi.org/10.1016/j.jpubeco.2010.11.009

Hattie, J., Hodis, F. A., & Kang, S. H. K. (2020). Theories of motivation: Integration and ways forward. *Contemporary Educational Psychology, 61*, Article 101865. https://doi.org/10.1016/j.cedpsych.2020.101865

Hautz, H. (2022). The 'conduct of conduct' of VET teachers: Governmentality and teacher professionalism. *Journal of Vocational Education & Training, 74*(2), 210–227. https://doi.org/10.1080/13636820.2020.1754278

Herman, J. L., & Linn, R. L. (2014). New assessments new rigor. *Educational Leadership, 71*(6), 34–37.

Hilton, G., Flores, M. A., & Niklasson, L. (2013). Teacher quality, professionalism and professional development: Findings from a European project. *Teacher Development, 17*(4), 431–447. https://doi.org/10.1080/13664530.2013.800743

Hordern, J., Muller, J., & Deng, Z. (2021). Towards powerful educational knowledge? Addressing the challenges facing educational foundations, curriculum theory and *Didaktik. Journal of Curriculum Studies, 53*(2), 143–152. https://doi.org/10.1080/00220272.2021.1891575

Howard, S. K., Tondeur, J., Siddiq, F., & Scherer, R. (2021). Ready, set, go! Profiling teachers' readiness for online teaching in secondary education. *Technology, Pedagogy & Education, 30*(1), 141–158. https://doi.org/10.1080/1475939X.2020.1839543

Huang, T., & Wiseman, A. W. (2011). The landscape of principal leadership development in mainland China: An analysis of Chinese and English research. *International Perspectives on Education and Society, 15*, 125–151. https://doi.org/10.1108/S1479-3679(2011)0000015009

Ingersoll, R. M., & Strong, M. (2011). The impact of induction and mentoring programs for beginning teachers: A critical review of the research. *Review of Educational Research, 81*(2), 201–233. https://doi.org/10.3102/0034654311403323

Ingvarson, L., Reid, K., Buckley, S., Kleinhenz, E., Masters, G., & Rowley, G. (2014). *Best practice teacher education programs and Australia's own programs*. Canberra Department of Education.

Ingvarson, L., & Rowe, K. (2008). Conceptualising and evaluating teacher quality: Substantive and methodological issues. *Australian Journal of Education, 52*(1), 5–35. https://doi.org/10.1177/0004944 10805200102

Irnidayanti, Y., Maulana, R., Helms-Lorenz, M., & Fadhilah, N. (2020). Relationship between teaching motivation and teaching behaviour of secondary education teachers in Indonesia. *Journal for the Study of Education and Development, 43*(2), 271–308. https://doi.org/10.1080/02103702.2020.1722413

Jha, A. S. (2011). Teacher empowerment and institutional effectiveness in teacher education. *Journal on School Educational Technology, 6*(3), 49–56. https://doi.org/10.26634/jsch.6.3.1378

Jiang, R., Kleer, R., & Piller, F. T. (2017). Predicting the future of additive manufacturing: A Delphi study on economic and societal implications of 3D printing for 2030. *Technological Forecasting and Social Change, 117*, 84–97. https://doi.org/10.1016/j.techfore.2017.01.006

Johnson, B., Down, B., Le Cornu, R., Peters, J., Sullivan, A., Pearce, J., & Hunter, J. (2014). Promoting early career teacher resilience: a framework for understanding and acting. *Teachers and Teaching, 20*(5), 530–546. https://doi.org/10.1080/13540602.2014.937957

Kabir, M. (2023). *Teachers for all: Improving primary school teacher deployment in Zambia*. United Nations Children's Fund Office of Research - Innocenti. https://www.unicef.org/innocenti/reports/teachers-for-all-zambia

Kane, M. (2012). Validating score interpretations and uses. *Language Testing, 29*(1), 3–17. https://doi.org/10.1177/0265532211417210

Karaolis, A., & Philippou, G. N. (2019). Teachers' professional identity. In M. S. Hannula, G. C. Leder, F. Morselli, M. Vollstedt, & Q. Zhang (Eds.), *Affect and mathematics education: Fresh perspectives on motivation, engagement, and identity* (pp. 397–419). Springer Open. https://doi.org/10.1007/978-3-030-13761-8_18

Karsenti, T., & Collin, S. (2013). Why are new teachers leaving the profession? Results of a Canada-wide survey. *Education, 3*(3), 141–149.

Keamy, R. K., & Selkrig, M. (2021). Interrupting practice traditions: using readers' theatre to show the impact of a nationally mandated assessment task on initial teacher educators' work. *Teaching Education, 33*(4), 419–433. https://doi.org/10.1080/10476210.2021.1951198

Keese, J., Waxman, H., & Kelly, L. J. (2022). Ready and able? Perceptions of confidence and teaching support for first-year alternatively certified teachers. *The Teacher Educator, 57*(3), 280–303. https://doi.org/10.1080/08878730.2021.2003496

Kelley, K., Clark, B., Brown, V., & Sitzia, J. (2003). Good practice in the conduct and reporting of survey research. *International Journal for Quality in Health Care, 15*(3), 261–266. https://doi.org/10.1093/intqhc/mzg031

Kellmereit, B. (2015). Focus groups. *International Journal of Sales, Retailing & Marketing, 4*(9), 42–52.

Klassen, R. M., Durksen, T. L., Al Hashmi, W., Kim, L. E., Longden, K., Metsäpelto, R.-L., Poikkeus, A.-M., & Györi, J. G. (2018). National context and teacher characteristics: Exploring the critical non-cognitive attributes of novice teachers in four countries. *Teaching and Teacher Education, 72*, 64–74. https://doi.org/10.1016/j.tate.2018.03.001

Klassen, R. M., & Tze, V. M. C. (2014). Teachers' self-efficacy, personality, and teaching effectiveness: A meta-analysis. *Educational Research Review, 12*, 59–76. https://doi.org/10.1016/j.edurev.2014.06.001

Knight, P., Tait, J., & Yorke, M. (2006). The professional learning of teachers in higher education. *Studies in Higher Education, 31*(3), 319–339. https://doi.org/10.1080/03075070600680786

Knoell, C., Harshbarger, D., Kracl, C., & Crow, S. (2015). Do you think like a fifth-grader? Exploring the teacher characteristics of importance to students from two diverse elementary schools in a rural Midwestern community. *International Journal of Psychology: Biopsychosocial Approach, 17*, 39–56. https://doi.org/10.7220/2345-024X.17.3

Korthagen, F., & Vasalos, A. (2005). Levels in reflection: Core reflection as a means to enhance professional growth. *Teachers and Teaching, 11*(1), 47–71. https://doi.org/10.1080/1354060042000337093

Kosnik, C., Rowsell, J., Williamson, P., Simon, R., & Beck, C. (Eds.). (2013). *Literacy teacher educators: Preparing teachers for a changing world*. Sense Publishers.

Koster, B., Brekelmans, M., Korthagen, F., & Wubbels, T. (2005). Quality requirements for teacher educators. *Teaching and Teacher Education, 21*(2), 157–176. https://doi.org/10.1016/j.tate.2004.12.004

Lambersky, J. (2016). Understanding the human side of school leadership: Principals' impact on teachers' morale, self-efficacy, stress, and commitment. *Leadership and Policy in Schools, 15*(4), 379–405. https://doi.org/10.1080/15700763.2016.1181188

Landis, J. R., & Koch, G. G. (1977). The measurement of observer agreement for categorical data. *Biometrics, 33*(1), 159–174. https://doi.org/10.2307/2529310

Larsen, C. M., Terkelsen, A. S., Carlsen, A.-M. F., & Kristensen, H. K. (2019). Methods for teaching evidence-based practice: A scoping review. *BMC Medical Education, 19*, Article 259. https://doi.org/10.1186/s12909-019-1681-0

Lauermann, F., & Karabenick, S. A. (2011). Taking teacher responsibility into account(ability): Explicating its multiple components and theoretical status. *Educational Psychologist, 46*(2), 122–140. https://doi.org/10.1080/00461520.2011.558818

Leavy, P. L. (2007). The practice of feminist oral history and focus group interviews. In S. N. Hesse-Biber & P. L. Leavy (Eds.), *Feminist research practice* (pp. 149–186). SAGE. https://doi.org/10.4135/9781412984270

Leggio, J., & Terras, K. (2019). An investigation of the qualities, knowledge, and skills of effective teachers for students with emotional/behavioral disorders: The teacher perspective. *The Journal of Special Education Apprenticeship, 8*(1), Article 2. https://doi.org/10.58729/2167-3454.1082

Leijen, Ä., Pedaste, M., & Lepp, L. (2020). Teacher agency following the ecological model: How it is achieved and how it could be strengthened by different types of reflection. *British Journal of Educational Studies*, *68*(3), 295–310. https://doi.org/10.1080/00071005.2019.1672855

Lester, J. N., Lochmiller, C. R., & Gabriel, R. (2016). Locating and applying critical discourse analysis within education policy: An introduction. *Education Policy Analysis Archives*, *24*, Article 102. https://doi.org/10.14507/epaa.24.2768

Levac, D., Colquhoun, H., & O'Brien, K. K. (2010). Scoping studies: Advancing the methodology. *Implementation Science*, *5*, Article 69. https://doi.org/10.1186/1748-5908-5-69

Longmuir, F. (2023). Leading in lockdown: Community, communication and compassion in response to the COVID-19 crisis. *Educational Management, Administration & Leadership*, *51*(5), 1014–1030. https://doi.org/10.1177/17411432211027634

Longmuir, F., Windsor, S., & Loeb, I. H. (2021). Disrupted and challenged learning practices: Students' experiences of 2020 as their final year of secondary schooling. *International Journal of Educational Research*, *110*, Article 101879. https://doi.org/10.1016/j.ijer.2021.101879

Lu, L. (2012). *A validation framework for automatic essay scoring systems* [Unpublished doctoral dissertation]. Wollongong University.

Maisuria, A., Roberts, N., Long, R., & Danechi, S. (2023). *Teacher recruitment and retention in England*. House of Commons Library. https://researchbriefings.files.parliament.uk/documents/CBP-7222/CBP-7222.pdf

Manasia, L., Ianos, M. G., & Chicioreanu, T. D. (2020). Pre-service teacher preparedness for fostering education for sustainable development: An empirical analysis of central dimensions of teaching readiness. *Sustainability*, *12*(1), Article 166. https://doi.org/10.3390/su12010166

Mansfield, C., Beltman, S., & Price, A. (2014). 'I'm coming back again!' The resilience process of early career teachers. *Teachers and Teaching*, *20*(5), 547–567. https://doi.org/10.1080/13540602.2014.937958

Manuel, J., & Carter, D. (2016). Sustaining hope and possibility: Early-career English teachers' perspectives on their first years of teaching. *English in Australia*, *51*(1), 91–103. https://doi.org/10.3316/informit.329597072811897

Martin, A. D., & Strom, K. J. (2016). Toward a linguistically responsive teacher identity: An empirical review of the literature. *International Multilingual Research Journal*, *10*(4), 239–253. https://doi.org/10.1080/19313152.2016.1189799

Marzano, R., Marzano, J., & Pickering, D. (2003). *Classroom management that works*. McGraw-Hill. https://perino.pbworks.com/f/4%20CLM-Basic-Text.pdf

Masters, G. N., & Forster, M. (1996). *Progress maps: Assessment resource kit*. Australian Council for Educational Research. https://research.acer.edu.au/ark/3

Mays, N., Pope, C., & Popay, J. (2005). *Details of approaches to synthesis – A methodological appendix to the paper: Systematically reviewing qualitative and quantitative evidence to inform management and policy making in the health field*. Canadian Health Services Research Foundation/ NHS Service Delivery and Organisation R&D Programme. https:// core.ac.uk/reader/13112440

McColskey, W., Stronge, J. H., Ward, T. J., Tucker, P. D., Howard, B., Lewis, K., & Hindman, J. L. (2006). *Teacher effectiveness, student achievement, & national board certified teachers: A comparison of national board certified teachers and non-national board certified teachers: Is there a difference in teacher effectiveness and student achievement?* The National Board for Professional Teaching Standards.

McGraw, A., Keamy, R. K., Kriewaldt, J., Brandenburg, R., Walker, R., & Crane, N. (2021). Collaboratively designing a national, mandated teaching performance assessment in a multi-university consortium: Leadership, dispositions and tensions. *Australian Journal of Teacher Education, 46*(5), 40–53.

McNamara, J. F. (1993). Ethical guidelines in survey research. *International Journal of Educational Reform, 2*(1), 96–101. https://doi.org/ 10.1177/105678799300200114

McNamara, O., & Murray, J. (2013). *The School Direct programme and its implications for research informed teacher education and teacher educators*. Higher Education Academy.

McPherson, A., Lampert, J., & Burnett, B. (2024). A summary of initiatives to address teacher shortages in hard-to-staff schools in the Anglosphere. *Asia-Pacific Journal of Teacher Education, 52*(3), 332–349. https://doi.org/10.1080/1359866X.2024.2323936

Messick, S. (1975). The standard problem: Meaning and values in measurement and evaluation. *American Psychologist, 30*, 955–966. https:// doi.org/10.1037/0003-066X.30.10.955

Messick, S. (1989). Validity. In R. L. Linn (Ed.), *Educational measurement* (3rd ed., pp. 13–103). American Council on Education.

Millar, K., Tomkins, S., Thorstensen, E., Mepham, B., & Kaiser, M. (2006). *Ethical Delphi manual*. LEI.

Mohamed, M., Ab Rashid, R., & Harb Alqaruouti, M. (2022). Conceptualizing the complexity of reflective practice in education. *Frontiers in Psychology, 13*, Article 1008234 https://doi.org/10.3389/fpsyg.2022. 1008234

Mohamed, Z., Valcke, M., & De Wever, B. (2017). Are they ready to teach? Student teachers' readiness for the job with reference to teacher competence frameworks. *Journal of Education for Teaching, 43*(2), 151–170. https://doi.org/10.1080/02607476.2016.1257509

Moon, J. A. (1999). *Reflection in learning and professional development: Theory and practice*. Routledge. https://doi.org/10.4324/9780203822296

Moore, A., & Clarke, M. (2016). 'Cruel optimism': Teacher attachment to professionalism in an era of performativity. *Journal of Education Policy, 31*(5), 666–677. https://doi.org/10.1080/02680939.2016.1160293

Morrison, A., Rigney, L.-I., Hattam, R., & Diplock, A. (2019). *Toward an Australian culturally responsive pedagogy: A narrative review of the literature*. University of South Australia. https://apo.org.au/node/262951

Morrison, C. M. (2013). Teacher identity in the early career phase: Trajectories that explain and influence development. *Australian Journal of Teacher Education, 38*(4), 91–107. https://doi.org/10.14221/ajte.2013v38n4.5

Muijs, D., & Reynolds, D. (2002). Teachers' beliefs and behaviours: What really matters? *The Journal of Classroom Interaction, 37*(2), 3–15. https://files.eric.ed.gov/fulltext/EJ1100408.pdf

Munn, Z., Peters, M. D. J., Stern, C., Tufanaru, C., McArthur, A., & Aromataris, E. (2018). Systematic review or scoping review? Guidance for authors when choosing between a systematic or scoping review approach. *BMC Medical Research Methodology, 18.* Article 143 https://doi.org/10.1186/s12874-018-0611-x

Murphy, K. R., & Davidshofer, C. O. (2001). *Psychological testing: Principles and applications.* Prentice Hall.

Naisola-Ruiter, V. (2022). The Delphi technique: A tutorial. *Research in Hospitality Management, 12*(1), 91–97. https://doi.org/10.1080/22243534.2022.2080942

National Board for Professional Teaching Standards. (2016). *What teachers should know and be able to do.* https://www.nbpts.org/wp-content/uploads/2017/07/what_teachers_should_know.pdf

National Center on Education and the Economy. (2016). Singapore: A teaching model for the 21st century. In *Empowered educators: How high-performing systems shape teaching quality around the world* (pp. 1–15). http://ncee.org/wp-content/uploads/2017/02/SingaporeCountryBrief.pdf

Neumann, M. M., & Tillott, S. (2022). Why should teachers cultivate resilience through mindfulness? *Journal of Psychologists and Counsellors in Schools, 32,* 3–14. https://doi.org/10.1017/jgc.2021.23

Newberry, M. (2010). Identified phases in the building and maintenance of positive teacher-student relationships. *Teaching and Teacher Education, 26,* 1695–1703. https://doi.org/10.1016.j.tate.2010.06.022

Nichols, S. L., Schutz, P. A., Rodgers, K., & Bilica, K. (2016). Early career teachers' emotion and emerging teacher identities. *Teachers and Teaching, 23*(4), 406–421. https://doi.org/10.1080/13540602.2016.1211099

Nowell, L. S., Norris, J. M., White, D. E., & Moules, N. J. (2017). Thematic analysis: Striving to meet the trustworthiness criteria. *International Journal of Qualitative Methods, 16,* 1–13. https://doi.org/10.1177/1609406917733847

O'Brien, K., Wilkins, A., Zack, E., & Solomon, P. (2010). Scoping the field: Identifying key research priorities in HIV and rehabilitation. *AIDS and Behavior, 14*(2), 448–458. https://doi.org/10.1007/s10461-009-9528-z

Oney, E., & Oksuzoglu-Guven, G. (2015). Confidence: A critical review of the literature and an alternative perspective for general and specific self-confidence. *Psychological Reports: Mental & Physical Health, 116*(1), 149–163. https://doi.org/10.2466/07.PR0.116k14w0

Organisation for Economic Co-operation and Development. (2001). Teachers for tomorrow's schools: Analysis of the world education indicators. https://unesdoc.unesco.org/ark:/48223/pf0000124265

Organisation for Economic Co-operation and Development. (2005). Teachers matter: Attracting, developing and retaining effective teachers. https://doi.org/10.1787/9789264018044-en

Organisation for Economic Co-operation and Development. (2021). The state of school education: One year into the COVID pandemic. https://doi.org/10.1787/201dde84-en

Pakistani Government Ministry of Education. (2009). *National professional standards for teachers in Pakistan.* https://www.nacte.org.pk/assets/download/NationalProfessionalStandardsforTeachersinPakistan.pdf

Panayiotou, A., Kyriakides, L., Creemers, B., McMahon, L., Vanlaar, G., Pfeifer, M., Rekalidou, G., & Bren, M. (2014). Teacher behavior and student outcomes: Results of a European study. *Educational Assessment, Evaluation and Accountability, 26*(1), 73–93. https://doi.org/10.1007/s11092-013-9182-x

Paniagua, A., & Sánchez-Martí, A. (2018). Early career teachers: Pioneers triggering innovation or compliant professionals? *OECD Education Working Papers, 190.* https://doi.org/10.1787/4a7043f9-en

Park, K., Park, N., Heo, W., & Gustafson, K. (2019). What prompts college students to participate in online surveys? *International Education Studies, 12*(1), 69–79. https://doi.org/10.5539/ies.v12n1p69

Park, S., & Oliver, J. S. (2008). Revisiting the conceptualisation of pedagogical content knowledge (PCK): PCK as a conceptual tool to understand teachers as professionals. *Research in Science Education, 38*(3), 261–284. https://doi.org/10.1007/s11165-007-9049-6

Paul, L., Louden, B., Elliott, M., & Scott, D. (2021). *Next steps: Report of the Quality Initial Teacher Education review.* Australian Government. https://www.education.gov.au/quality-initial-teacher-education-review/resources/next-steps-report-quality-initial-teacher-education-review

Pham, M. T., Rajić, A., Greig, J. D., Sargeant, J. M., Papadopoulos, A., & McEwen, S. A. (2014). A scoping review of scoping reviews: Advancing the approach and enhancing the consistency. *Research Synthesis Methods, 5*(4), 371–385. https://doi.org/10.1002/jrsm.1123

Phillips, A. C., Lewis, L. K., McEvoy, M. P., Galipeau, J., Glasziou, P., Hammick, M., Moher, D., Tilson, J. K., & Williams, M. T. (2014). A Delphi survey to determine how educational interventions for evidence-based practice should be reported: Stage 2 of the development of a reporting guideline. *BMC Medical Education, 14,* Article 159. https://doi.org/10.1186/1472-6920-14-159

Planinic, M., Boone, W. J., Susac, A., & Ivanjek, L. (2019). Rasch analysis in physics education research: Why measurement matters. *Physical Review Physics Education Research, 15*(2), Article 020111. https://doi.org/10.1103/PhysRevPhysEducRes.15.020111

Pollock, K., & Briscoe, P. (2019). School principals' understandings of student difference and diversity and how these understandings influence their work. *International Journal of Educational Management, 34*(3), 518–534. https://doi.org/10.1108/IJEM-07-2019-0243

Prosina, O., Kyrychenko, M., Sergeieva, L., Ivchenko, T., & Fedorova, Y. (2024). Exploration of pedagogical staff readiness for professional transformation: Analysis of synchronous online focus group (SOFG) study results. *African Journal of Applied Research, 10*(1), 400–417. https://doi.org/10.26437/ajar.v10i1.711

Rea, L. M., & Parker, R. A. (2014). *Designing and conducting survey research: A comprehensive guide.* John Wiley & Sons.

Reeves, T. D., & Marbach-Ad, G. (2016). Contemporary test validity in theory and practice: A primer for discipline-based education researchers. *CBE Life Sciences Education, 15*(1), 1–9. https://doi.org/10.1187/cbe.15-08-0183

Rinaldo, V., Denig, S., Sheeran, T., Vermette, P., & Smith, R. M. (2009). Validly and reliably assessing teacher candidate dispositions toward teaching. *Teacher Education & Practice, 22*(2), 165–179.

Rizvi, F., & Lingard, B. (2000). Globalization and education: Complexities and contingencies. *Educational Theory, 50*(4), 419–426. https://doi.org/10.1111/j.1741-5446.2000.00419.x

Roberts, L., & Allen, P. (2012). Student perspectives on the value of research participation. In S. McCarthy, K. L. Dickson, J. Cranney, A. Trapp, & V. Karandashev (Eds.), *Teaching psychology around the world* (Vol. 3, pp. 198–211). Cambridge Scholars Publishing. http://hdl.handle.net/20.500.11937/34846

Roberts, L. D., & Allen, P. J. (2015). Exploring ethical issues associated with using online surveys in educational research. *Educational Research and Evaluation, 21*(2), 95–108. https://doi.org/10.1080/13803611.2015.1024421

Rodgers, C. (2002). Defining reflection: Another look at John Dewey and reflective thinking. *Teachers College Record, 104*(4), 842–866. https://doi.org/10.1111/1467-9620.00181

Rogers, P. (2024). Best practices for your confirmatory factor analysis: A JASP and *lavaan* tutorial. *Behavior Research Methods, 56*, 6634–6654. https://doi.org/10.3758/s13428-024-02375-7

Rogers, R., Malancharuvil-Berkes, E., Mosley, M., Hui, D., & O'Garro Joseph, G. (2005). Critical discourse analysis in education: A review of the literature. *Review of Educational Research, 75*(3), 365–416. https://doi.org/10.3102/00346543075003365

Roorda, D. L., Koomen, H. M. Y., Spilt, J. L., & Oort, F. J. (2011). The influence of affective teacher–student relationships on students' school engagement and achievement: A meta-analytic approach. *Review of Educational Research, 81*(4), 493–529. https://doi.org/10.3102/0034654311421793

Roose, I., Vantieghemb, W., Vanderlindec, R., & Van Avermaet, P. (2019). Beliefs as filters for comparing inclusive classroom situations. Connecting teachers' beliefs about teaching diverse learners to their noticing of inclusive classroom characteristics in videoclips. *Contemporary Educational Psychology, 56*, 140–151. https://doi.org/10.1016/j.cedpsych.2019.01.002

Rowan, L., Bourke, T., L'Estrange, L., Brownlee, J. L., Ryan, M., Walker, S., & Churchward, P. (2021). How does initial teacher education research frame the challenge of preparing future teachers for student diversity in schools? A systematic review of literature. *Review of Educational Research, 91*(1), 112–158. https://doi.org/10.3102/00346543 20979171

Rowe, E. E., & Skourdoumbis, A. (2019). Calling for 'urgent national action to improve the quality of initial teacher education': The reification of evidence and accountability in reform agendas. *Journal of Education Policy, 34*(1), 44–60. https://doi.org/10.1080/02680939.2017. 1410577

Sachs, J. (2000). Rethinking the practice of teacher professionalism. In C. Day, A. Fernandez, T. E. Hauge, & J. Moller (Eds.), *The life and work of teachers: International perspectives in changing times* (pp. 75–88). Routledge Falmer.

Sachs, J. (2013). Teacher professional standards: A policy strategy to control, regulate or enhance the teaching profession? In N. Bascia, A. Cumming, A. Datnow, K. Leithwood, & D. Livingstone (Eds.), *International handbook of educational policy* (pp. 579–592). Springer.

Sadler, D. R. (1987). Specifying and promulgating achievement standards. *Oxford Review of Education, 13*(2), 191–209. https://doi.org/10.1080/ 0305498870130207

Santoro, N., & Kennedy, A. (2016). How is cultural diversity positioned in teacher professional standards? An international analysis. *Asia-Pacific Journal of Teacher Education, 44*(3), 208–223. https://doi.org/10.1080/1 359866X.2015.1081674

Schön, D. A. (1983). *The reflective practitioner: How professionals think in action.* Basic Books.

Schuck, S., Aubusson, P., Buchanan, J., Varadharajan, M., & Burke, P. F. (2018). The experiences of early career teachers: New initiatives and old problems. *Professional Development in Education, 44*(2), 209–221. https://doi.org/10.1080/19415257.2016.1274268

Scott, C., Medaugh, M., Potter, R. F., Matthes, J., & Davis, C. S. (2017). Axial coding. In J. Matthes (Ed.), *The International encyclopedia of communication research methods* (pp. 1–2). John Wiley & Sons. https:// doi.org/10.1002/9781118901731.iecrm0012

Scott, T. M., Jolivette, K., Ennis, R. P., & Hirn, R. G. (2012). Defining "effectiveness" for students with E/BD: Teacher, instruction, and management variables. *Beyond Behavior, 22*(1), 3–6. https://doi.org/10. 1177/107429561202200102

Sezer, S., Karabacak, N., Kucuk, M., & Korkmaz, I. (2020). School administrators' opinions related to the values that should be gained to classroom teachers through in-service training. *Eurasian Journal of Educational Research, 20*(86), 175–196. https://doi.org/10.14689/ejer. 2020.86.9

Shulman, L. S. (1987). Knowledge and teaching: Foundations of the new reform. *Harvard Educational Review, 57*(1), 1–22. https://doi.org/10. 17763/haer.57.1.j463w79r56455411

Sim, J. (1998). Collecting and analysing qualitative data: Issues raised by the focus group. *Journal of Advanced Nursing, 28*(2), 345–352. https://doi.org/10.1046/j.1365-2648.1998.00692.x

Simpson, A., Day, C., Goulding, J., & Asha, J. (2022). Australian teachers' perceptions of effectiveness in a performative culture. *Teaching and Teacher Education, 109*, Article 103542. https://doi.org/10.1016/j.tate.2021.103542

Simpson, A., Sang, G., Wood, J., Wang, Y., & Ye, B. (2018). A dialogue about teacher agency: Australian and Chinese perspectives. *Teaching and Teacher Education, 75*, 316–326. https://doi.org/10.1016/j.tate.2018.07.002

Sinha, I. P., Smyth, R. L., & Williamson, P. R. (2011). Using the Delphi technique to determine which outcomes to measure in clinical trials: Recommendations for the future based on a systematic review of existing studies. *PLoS Medicine, 8*(1), Article e1000393. https://doi.org/10.1371/journal.pmed.1000393

Smith, D. (2014). Fostering collective ethical capacity within the teaching profession. *Journal of Academic Ethics, 12*(4), 271–286. https://doi.org/10.1007/s10805-014-9218-y

Smith, M. K., Jones, F. H. M., Gilbert, S. L., & Wieman, C. E. (2013). The classroom observation protocol for undergraduate STEM (COPUS): A new instrument to characterise university STEM classroom practices. CBE *Life Sciences Education, 12*, 618–627. https://doi.org/10.1187/cbe.13-08-0154

Stacey, M., Talbot, D., Buchanan, J., & Mayer, D. (2019). The development of an Australian teacher performance assessment: Lessons from the international literature. *Asia-Pacific Journal of Teacher Education, 48*(5), 508–519. https://doi.org/10.1080/1359866X.2019.1669137

Stets, J., & Burke, P. (2000). Identity theory and social identity theory. *Social Psychology Quarterly, 63*(3), 224–237. https://doi.org/10.2307/2695870

Stets, J. E., & Burke, P. J. (2014). Emotions and identity nonverification. *Social Psychology Quarterly, 77*(4), 387–410. https://doi.org/10.1177/0190272514533708

Stets, J. E., & Serpe, R. T. (2013). Identity theory. In J. DeLamater & A. Ward (Eds.), *Handbook of social psychology* (pp. 31–60). Springer. https://doi.org/10.1007/978-94-007-6772-0_2

Stewart, S., Stratford, E., & te Riele, K. (2021). A trialectical approach to understanding 'classroom readiness' for teaching literacy. *Studies in Continuing Education, 43*(3), 311–327. https://doi.org/10.1080/0158037X.2021.1900096

Stokking, K., Leenders, F., De Jong, J., & Van Tartwijk, J. (2003). From student to teacher: Reducing practice shock and early dropout in the teaching profession. *European Journal of Teacher Education, 26*(3), 329–350. https://doi.org/10.1080/0261976032000128175

Straková, J., Simonová, J., & Greger, D. (2018). Improving mathematics results: Does teachers' academic optimism matter? A study of lower secondary schools. *School Effectiveness and School Improvement, 29*(3), 446–463. https://doi.org/10.1080/09243453.2018.1446449

Strong, M. (2011). *The highly qualified teacher: What is teacher quality and how do we measure it?* Teachers College Press.

Stronge, J. (2007). *Qualities of effective teachers* (2nd ed.). ASCD.

Sullivan, A., Johnson, B., Simons, M., & Tippett, N. (2021). When performativity meets agency: How early career teachers struggle to reconcile competing agendas to become 'quality' teachers. *Teachers and Teaching, 27*(5), 388–403. https://doi.org/10.1080/13540602.2020.1806050

Taylor, E. (2020). We agree, don't we? The Delphi method for health environments research. *HERD: Health Environments Research & Design Journal, 13*(1), 11–23. https://doi.org/10.1177/1937586719887709

Tebaldi, C. (2024). Privatizing creation: Neoliberal creativity in the language classroom. *Critical Inquiry in Language Studies, 21*(2), 177–201. https://doi.org/10.1080/15427587.2023.2219455

Teng, S., & Alonzo, D. (2023). Critical review of the Australian Professional Standards for Teachers: Where are the non-cognitive skills? *International Journal of Instruction, 16*(1), 605–624. https://doi.org/10.29333/iji.2023.16134a

The Teaching Council. (2016). *Code of professional conduct.* https://www.teachingcouncil.ie/fitness-to-teach/updated-code-of-professional-conduct/

Thomas, S. (2008). Leading for quality: Questions about quality and leadership in Australia. *Journal of Education Policy, 23*(3), 323–334. https://doi.org/10.1080/02680930801923807

Tichnor-Wagner, A., Parkhouse, H., Glazier, J., & Cain, J. M. (2016). Expanding approaches to teaching for diversity and social justice in K-12 education: Fostering global citizenship across the content areas. *Education Policy Analysis Archives, 24*(59), 1–30. https://doi.org/10.14507/epaa.24.2138

Tognolini, J. (2018). Assessing skills and measuring performance of students on skills that are aligned with the needs of the 21st Century: A practical example. *Proceedings of the Second Universitas Riau International Conference on Educational Sciences,* 1–10.

Tognolini, J., & Davidson, M. (2013). Assessment, standards-referencing and standard setting. In M. M. C. Mok (Ed.), *Self-directed learning-oriented assessment in the Asia-Pacific* (pp. 23–42). Springer.

Tognolini, J., & Stanley, G. (2007). Standards-based assessment: A tool and means to the development of human capital and capacity building in education. *Australian Journal of Education, 51*(2), 129–145. https://doi.org/10.1177/000494410705100203

Toom, A. (2019). Shaping teacher identities and agency for the profession: Contextual factors and surrounding communities. *Teachers and Teaching, 25*(8), 915–917. https://doi.org/10.1080/13540602.2019.1703619

Torrance, D., & Forde, C. (2017). Redefining what it means to be a teacher through professional standards: Implications for continuing teacher education. *European Journal of Teacher Education, 40*(1), 110–126. https://doi.org/10.1080/02619768.2016.1246527

Tschannen-Moran, M., & Woolfolk Hoy, A. (2007). The differential antecedents of self-efficacy beliefs of novice and experienced teachers.

*Teaching and Teacher Education, 23*(6), 944–956. https://doi.org/10. 1016/j.tate.2006.05.003

UK Government Department for Education. (2011). *Teachers' standards: Guidance for school leaders, school staff and governing bodies.* https:// assets.publishing.service.gov.uk/media/61b73d6c8fa8f50384489c9a/ Teachers__Standards_Dec_2021.pdf

United Nations. (2022). *United Nations Transforming Education Summit discussion paper – Thematic Action Track 3: Teachers, teaching and the teaching profession.* https://media.unesco.org/sites/default/files/webform/ ed3002/Thematic%2520Action%2520Track%25203%2520teachers%2520 discussion%2520paper%2520July%25202022.pdf

United Nations Educational Scientific and Cultural Organization. (2015). *Education 2030: Incheon declaration and framework for action for the implementation of sustainable development goal 4: Ensure inclusive and equitable quality education and promote lifelong learning opportunities for all.* https://unesdoc.unesco.org/ark:/48223/pf0000245656

United Nations Educational Scientific and Cultural Organization. (2022, March 21). *The transforming education summit advisory committee convenes at UNESCO* [Press release]. https://www.unesco.org/en/articles/ transforming-education-summit-advisory-committee-convenes-unesco

Van der Vaart, R., Witting, M., Riper, H., Kooistra, L., Bohlmeijer, E. T., & van Gemert-Pijnen, L. J. (2014). Blending online therapy into regular face-to-face therapy for depression: Content, ratio and preconditions according to patients and therapists using a Delphi study. *BMC Psychiatry, 14*, Article 355. https://doi.org/10.1186/s12888-014-0355-z

van Dijk, T. A. (2015). Critical discourse analysis. In D. Tannen, H. E. Hamilton, & D. Schiffrin (Eds.), *The handbook of discourse analysis* (2nd ed., pp. 466–485). John Wiley & Sons. https://doi.org/10.1002/ 9781118584194.ch22

van Es, E. A., & Sherin, M. G. (2002). Learning to notice: Scaffolding new teachers' interpretations of classroom interactions. *Journal of Technology and Teacher Education, 10*(4), 571–595.

Van Selm, M., & Jankowski, N. W. (2006). Conducting online surveys. *Quality and Quantity, 40*, 435–456. https://doi.org/10.1007/s11135-005-8081-8

Van Zile-Tamsen, C. (2017). Using Rasch analysis to inform rating scale development. *Research in Higher Education, 58*(8), 922–933. https://doi. org/10.1007/s11162-017-9448-0

Virtanen, P., & Laine, A. (2021). Grounds for differences in motivation among Finnish student teachers and novice primary school teachers. *Issues in Education Research, 31*(1), 291–308. http://hdl.handle.net/ 10138/329399

Volman, M. (2005). A variety of roles for a new type of teacher: Educational technology and the teaching profession. *Teaching and Teacher Education, 21*(1), 15–31. https://doi.org/10.1016/j.tate.2004.11.003

von der Gracht, H. A. (2012). Consensus measurement in Delphi studies: Review and implications for future quality assurance. *Technological Forecasting and Social Change, 79*(8), 1525–1536. https://doi.org/10. 1016/j.techfore.2012.04.013

Watson, J., & Beswick, K. (2011). School pupil change associated with a continuing professional development programme for teachers. *Journal of Education for Teaching, 37*(1), 63–75. https://doi.org/10.1080/026074 76.2011.538273

Weingand, D. E. (1998). *Future-driven library marketing.* American Library Association.

White, D. E., Oelke, N. D., & Friesen, S. (2012). Management of a large qualitative data set: Establishing trustworthiness of the data. *International Journal of Qualitative Methods, 11*(3), 244–258. https://doi.org/10.1177/160940691201100305

White, K. M. (2020). Building strong teacher–child relationships in today's kindergarten classroom: Focusing on opportunities versus obstacles. *Journal of Early Childhood Research, 18*(3), 275–286. https://doi.org/10.1177/1476718X20938092

White, S. (2016). Teacher education research and education policy-makers: An Australian perspective. *Journal of Education for Teaching, 42*(2), 252–264. https://doi.org/10.1080/02607476.2016.1145369

Wilson, M., & Sloane, K. (2000). From principles to practice: An embedded assessment system. *Applied Measurement in Education, 13*(2), 181–208. https://doi.org/10.1207/S15324818AME1302_4

Wire, T. (2022). "They don't need to know that." Focus groups as a model for teacher-led research and curriculum consultation. *Practice, 4*(1), 42–55. https://doi.org/10.1080/25783858.2021.1896344

Wiswall, M. (2013). The dynamics of teacher quality. *Journal of Public Economics, 100*, 61–78. https://doi.org/10.1016/j.jpubeco.2013.01.006

Yuan, R., Zhang, J., & Yu, S. (2018). Understanding teacher collaboration processes from a complexity theory perspective: A case study of a Chinese secondary school. *Teachers and Teaching, 24*(5), 520–537. https://doi.org/10.1080/13540602.2018.1447458

Zavelevsky, E., & Lishchinsky, O. S. (2020). An ecological perspective of teacher retention: An emergent model. *Teaching and Teacher Education, 88*, Article 102965. https://doi.org/10.1016/j.tate.2019.102965

Zawacki-Richter, O. (2009). Research areas in distance education: A Delphi study. *International Review of Research in Open and Distributed Learning, 10*(3). https://doi.org/10.19173/irrodl.v10i3.674

Zeichner, K. M. (2005). A research agenda for teacher education. In M. Cochran-Smith & K. M. Zeichner (Eds.), *Studying teacher education: The report of the AERA panel on research and teacher education* (pp. 737–759). Routledge.

Ziljstra, A. H. (2015). *Early grade learning: The role of teacher-child interaction and tutor-assisted intervention* [Doctoral dissertation, Universiteit van Amsterdam]. http://dare.uva.nl/record/1/493800

# Index

For Product Safety Concerns and Information please contact our EU
representative  GPSR@taylorandfrancis.com
Taylor & Francis Verlag GmbH, Kaufingerstraße 24, 80331 München, Germany

www.ingramcontent.com/pod-product-compliance
Ingram Content Group UK Ltd.
Pitfield, Milton Keynes, MK11 3LW, UK
UKHW022305100726
473146UK00009B/337